On the publication of Tom Hart's last book, a novel called *The Aura and the Kingfisher*, the *Daily Telegraph* said: 'his eye for telling detail, his sensitive response to natural beauty, encourage one to look forward to his next book'.

Here it is. *Safe on a Seesaw* is a social documentary in which Tom Hart tells stories about the children we prefer to forget: the battered, the unwanted, those who end up in care; children such as Penny, whose neighbours gossip about her sleeping around, Lionel, who swallows cutlery, Amanda, who has spent five of her nine years locked in a room by her parents, and Dennis, an eight-year-old arsonist.

These pieces are interspersed with anecdotes from the author's own childhood in the north of England. They show how his own background has enabled him to become one of Britain's most successful and sympathetic social workers dealing with children. It is from his experience with children that these accounts come. Each is true and highly moving. Some are funny, some desperately sad. But together they form an impassioned plea for the better care of our young people – not only by the authorities but by parents, friends and teachers, and by the public.

SAFE ON A SEESAW
A Book of Children

Ω————————————————————

TOM HART

QUARTET BOOKS   LONDON

First published by Quartet Books Limited 1977
A member of the Namara Group
27 Goodge Street, London W1P 1FD

ISBN 0 7043 2089 4

Typesetting by Bedford Typesetters Ltd

Printed in Great Britain by litho at The Anchor Press Ltd
and bound by Wm Brendon & Son Ltd
both of Tiptree, Essex

For all those who work with
and care for
other people's children
– and for those who toil
in the field

PROLOGUE

Working with children makes you realize that growing old does not necessarily bring wisdom, that sometimes, as we grow older, we perhaps become more devious. Our honesty is qualified by not wishing to make ourselves seem foolish, we lie so as not to give offence and we profess to like that which we wholeheartedly detest. Children are not like this; they nearly always tell the truth. Children in care don't lie, they just express their hopes and their needs in fantasy, so creating worlds which will not be so painful. They do not indulge in believing in fairies and fairyland, as other children do, but create worlds of loving mothers and fathers, of families and homes which will be better than the fantasy home of the child sleeping in the next bed in the children's home. They judge the people with whom they live, they know what those people like and dislike and so tend to give them what it is they are wanting, but beneath all their pain and sorrow there is often to be found considerable humour, and now and again this humour bubbles to the surface, knocking out of us, for a brief moment, our adult pomposity and reducing us to a level which is, to the child, almost human.

For those of us fortunate enough to have experienced these moments in our working lives, the incidents remain vivid in memory. In time, when we look back – those of us who have worked in institutions of one kind or another, in children's homes, in what used to be called approved schools and remand homes, and the social workers in the field who bear such a large responsibility for the welfare of these children – when we look back at the children we have known, we remember the funny times together with the sad and we recall vividly, perhaps more vividly, the children who have gone through their lives suffering while we, who were caring for them, have not been able to meet their needs, perhaps have not understood what those needs were. Not because we did not care, but perhaps because we had neither the skills nor the knowledge, or, on occasions, the insight to help them to overcome their disabilities.

'Child care' is a term that is tossed about. 'Children in care', 'children's homes', 'foster children' – these are terms seen every day in the press, particularly when some child has had a traumatic experience, either due to our neglect, or because, again, we were unable to anticipate what the child's needs were. But the general public, the people who pay our salaries, have little idea what these children are like: they are not like the child clutching his teddy bear depicted in newspapers at Christmas to strike some chord at an emotional season and solicit donations or toys from those who see the picture. The child in care is real, with his pain, humour and courage.

In all the places where I have worked – children's homes, reception centres, remand homes – I have met these children, varying in age between two and eighteen years. Each one of them holds within him or herself their pain and anger, and is seeking someone who will understand, someone who will be prepared to hear them without passing moral judgement, without endeavouring to change their basic personalities, but who will accept some of their pain, anguish and anger, and be rewarded by their humour. These children suffer from a rare sickness, not physical or psychiatric, but a sickness of the soul. It is a sickness we know nothing about, for we have seldom experienced it ourselves, and those of us who have seldom know how to put into words what it is like to have what I believe to be the most painful of this world's afflictions . . . to have been denied what is basically everybody's birthright: to be able to live within a loving home, an ordinary home where the people help each other to overcome their afflictions, and where, in love, one forgives another and has an understanding of and a compassion for another member of the family's pain or inadequacy.

2

For all people are, I believe, deprived in some way or other, and only overcome their deprivation and adjust because of the love and understanding of those close to them, and because of the awareness of this love and the inward knowledge that each person has of their love for one another. Loneliness: the isolation of being separated from one's family and environment, to feel love and not have it returned, the despair of knowing that there is no one to whom you can turn or feel you belong. It was as a young boy that I first saw deprivation, but I didn't then know or understand what it was that I was looking at.

In the towns of the North, particularly in Lancashire and the West Riding of Yorkshire, there was an effort from 1931 onwards to clear out the slums by building huge estates of council houses. The labour that was needed, especially the hard labour, was imported from Ireland: hundreds of Irish navvies to dig the trenches and the footings of the houses all by hand, no mechanical excavators. For a shilling an hour perhaps it was cheaper. The men worked methodically, digging into the clay while gangers walked up and down like medieval slave masters making sure that their overlords got their shilling's worth.

On one such job my father was a civil engineer. He had an office: a wooden hut with a desk built on to the side for the drawings. In one corner of the hut was a stove that burnt coke, and a kettle. There were a number of these huts on the site for the various contractors, and as a boy I used to see an old man sweeping out the huts and making tea for the bosses on the job. Mick Cole was his name, but I don't know how old he was – the navvies were all very respectful to him as he got on with his work.

'Good morning, Mick,' you'd hear them call.

'Good morning, Peter.'

It was said that on a Monday morning he used to walk along the trenches where the men were digging and say, 'I didn't see you at Mass, Peter.'

'Oh sure, I went to such and such a church,' they would tell him, and Mick would nod his head. For many an hour I would see him working methodically, cleaning the offices, cleaning up the kettles and wheeling his barrow of coke. Sometimes he would sit and talk to me and tell me of all the places he had worked in

England, and all the jobs he had been on. He had a kind of pride in what he had done.

'And now I look after all the fine people,' he used to say with a laugh, moving a hand to indicate all the wooden hut offices.

When Sunday came he could be seen at Mass at eleven o'clock, and if you went at nine o'clock you'd see him up there on the altar. On Sunday he wore a blue serge suit, and I remember that his shirt then had a stiff front and a stiff winged collar and he wore a tie that was like a thin piece of black lace. He had a bowler hat obviously kept only for Sundays and holy days of obligation. At his waistcoat he also wore a gold watch-chain, and in the pocket was a half-hunter watch – his one great pride.

Mick was Mr Cole to me. I learnt that when I went on the job one day during the holidays and said, 'Hello, Mick.' A heavy hand fell on my shoulder and turned me round. 'Mr Cole to you,' said my father, 'and don't you forget it.'

For some reason this made me feel very ashamed and I apologized to Mr Cole. 'That was all right,' he said . . . it was only because I'd heard everyone else call him Mick.

Mick was kind to me. Occasionally I would see him at my home, talking to my mother and drinking tea. I never thought to ask why he was there; even now I don't know. While Mick was a man respected by all the men, he had a dignity which also gained him the respect of the men whose offices he tended. I never heard him swear, and, my father said, he'd never heard a man swear in front of Mick. He also told me that Mick always kept his missal in his pocket, yet never talked religion and liked his shilling on the horses.

I knew Mick for two or three years, and in a way he became part of a picture of my childhood: when I think back now to those periods, Mick always springs to mind.

It was one Thursday evening when there was a knock on our door and I went to answer it. An Irishman was standing there. 'Is your father in?' he asked.

'Yes. Come in.' I took him to my father.

'Hello, Michael. What can I do for you?'

'It's Mick, sir,' he said.

'What's the matter with Mick?'

'He's very ill, sir.'

'Where?'

'Down at where he stays,' said the man falteringly.

'I'll come with you,' said my father.

It was quite late, I remember, about nine o'clock. 'I've got a van from the job outside,' said the man. I looked at my father and he nodded. 'All right, if you want,' he said.

We drove down into the town, then through and into an area where I had never been. I knew that many of the Irishmen lived down here, and as we drove I could see, from the lights by the road, 'Toomey's Lodging House' and other people's lodging houses. We drove down a narrow street and at one side I could see a yard filled with bales of wool. The road was cobbled and the houses looked dirty. The doorways of the warehouses looked black and rather threatening. I looked at my father, who seemed to know what was going through my mind.

'It's all right,' he said.

The van pulled up outside a large building which had two large windows downstairs, half covered by a curtain but allowing the light to shine through the top half.

'Here it is,' said Michael.

I followed my father into an entrance hall. Inside there was a kind of window, the type where you get tickets at a railway station. There were stone floors and a stone staircase which went up to where there was a dim light above, and there was a man standing at the bottom of the stairs. He was a big man and seemed fat, his face looking white though his hands were red and rough. He had a blue-and-white butcher-type apron hanging over his arm.

'He's up the stairs,' he said in a broad West Riding dialect. 'I've had the doctor and he says he's not to be moved tonight. Anyway, it's not much use moving him.'

'Why not?' asked my father.

'He'd never get there.'

I stood behind my father and Michael and I suddenly realized what a big man Michael was and this made me feel less afraid. Michael half turned his head and stared down at me.

'It's all right,' he said as if he sensed my nervousness. I realized how quiet everywhere in this building appeared to be. We walked up the stone stairs, up two flights, then came to a big landing with two swing doors on one side. Michael nodded and we walked through.

We were in a corridor with lots of doors, and Michael went

towards one door that was partially open. Standing around in this corridor of doors were a number of men, all silent and all looking as if they were dressed in black, though this could have been my imagination or the dimness of the light. I recognized several of the men who worked on the job. I half smiled, and they smiled reassuringly back at me and put out their hands to rub my hair. We walked through a door into a cubicle which would be something like the size of a cell – about nine feet long and six feet wide.

There was a man already standing at the end of the bed. Mick's bowler hat was up on a shelf above the bed, and next to it, in a glass dish with a lid in it, was his stiff white collar, and I could just see the end of his black tie. He lay in the bed, quite still and very white. He looked older than any man I had ever seen then or have seen since.

'Good evening, Father,' said my father to the man standing at the end of the bed.

'Good evening,' he replied. 'He wanted you.'

My father went to the side of this black tubular iron bed. The sheets on it looked white and clean and he lay there with his arms resting on the covers. He was wearing a striped flannel shirt. Michael stood behind my father who sat and took old Mick's hand.

'Mick. Mick.'

Mick turned his head. 'It's yourself,' he said. 'It's good to see you.'

'It's good to see you, my friend,' said my father.

I craned my head round Michael and Mick saw me.

'You brought the boy.'

'Yes, I hope you don't mind, he wanted to come.'

Mick looked at me. 'No,' he said. 'No, it's good to have a young'n here at a time like this.'

'Is there something you want me to do, Mick?'

The old man nodded. My father looked at me and I left the room. Michael came with me, leaving my father and the priest alone in the room with Mick. How long they remained there it is difficult to remember now; to me, as a boy, it seemed a long time. Then the priest came out.

'You can go in now,' he said.

I noticed that the priest had his stole round his neck. He was taking it off, and he kissed it before he folded it up.

My father sat there with Mick, who opened his eyes and looked at him. 'It's getting late for you, sir,' he said.

'I'll stay, if you don't mind.'

'I wouldn't mind that at all,' said Mick.

I stood. I felt my legs beginning to ache and I leaned on the end of the bed, making the iron creak. My father looked at me. 'You'd better go home,' he said. 'Tell your mother I'll come when I can.'

'Can't I stay?'

'No, you'd better go.'

'I'll take you home,' said Michael.

'Thank you.'

We walked out of the room to the corridor where the men had been standing when we came in, but it was empty now. I walked down the stairs with this big Irishman and could feel his hand on my shoulder. Outside, the cold air seemed to chill me through.

'Are you all right?'

'Yes, I'm all right, Michael,' I said.

The road seemed to be packed with men, all men. I remember now that there were no women anywhere. The men stood silently in the street, down the sides, along the walls and in the doorways of the warehouses. I heard Michael say, 'You must let the boy through,' and one or two of them who knew me by name spoke to me, but all I could think of to say was, 'Hello.'

As we were half-way through the crowd a voice suddenly spoke, sounding loud.

'*Hail Mary, full of grace, the Lord is with thee. Blessed art thou amongst women and blessed is the fruit of thy womb, Jesus.*'

There was a moment's silence and then the voices of all these men suddenly answered.

'*Holy Mary, Mother of God, pray for us sinners now and at the hour of our death. Amen.*'

As a child, I felt an emotion it is easier to understand as I grow older. All the loneliness, the isolation, the feeling of exile and the deprivation echoed in their prayer for Mick Cole. All the fears and the loneliness of these men seemed to fill my mind, but, as a boy, I didn't fully realize; I could only sense the deep unhappiness that welled up out of these men. It must have been the same when slaves were transported to the Americas and their songs told of their

7

unhappiness. It was their prayer, their calling out to a woman for love and for comfort. In a profound sense, only a woman could have answered the prayers of these men.

I went home. Michael never spoke to me. He took me to the door and rang the bell; my mother came.

'He'll be back when he can, ma'am,' he said.

'Thank you, Michael.'

My mother gave me a hot drink. She asked no questions and I went to bed. When I saw my father the next morning, he told me Mick was dead.

The procession will still be remembered in that town by men of my age. There was no work done on the jobs that day. All the Irishmen gathered in the street outside the lodging house, and the small coffin was carried down the stairs and lifted on to the shoulders of the men. They carried Mick through the streets of the mill town for the whole four miles to the Catholic church. They filled the church. The coffin was taken in. The candles were lit and Mass was said. The responses came from deep within these men. A church full of men to weep for a man without a woman, to weep for a man to be buried in an alien land but not among, or by, an alien people.

So they carried Mick to the cemetery, and they buried him. I didn't see such isolation again, or sense such loss, deprivation and unhappiness, until many years later when I worked with truly deprived children, children who had only themselves to depend on. There is no other picture that I can give to explain deprivation. What is deprivation? What is loneliness? What is it to be an outcast, an isolate among millions? The death of Mick Cole is the nearest answer I can give.

1   DENNIS

It was late one Friday evening when I received a phone call from a social worker. He sounded a little out of breath.

'I have a hell of a problem,' he said. 'I have a boy in a school down in the country, a hellishly disturbed little boy and I've got to have him out of there by tomorrow morning.'

'Why . . . why tomorrow?' I asked.

'Well, it's a little difficult, he is not a bad kid at all really, he is disturbed but, you know, not really a bad kid.'

'Well, what's his problem?'

'He tends to worry people somewhat.'

'In what way?'

'Well, he does odd things which some people find disturbing; he tends to worry adults.'

'What's he done to worry the adults he is with now?'

'He never really liked the school, he never settled properly.'

'What . . . well, I gather he must have done something if he has to be moved in such a rush.'

'Well, I don't really think he meant it, but I'm afraid he has got to be moved, and I wondered if you would take him. I really do think we have got to have somebody take a look at this lad and see if we can find out what his difficulties are and do something about them. Will you take him?'

'Well, I suppose I will,' I said, 'but why does he have to move in such a hurry?'

9

'Does it make any difference?' asked the social worker.

'I suppose not, but it would be nice to know what he has done.'

There was a long pause on the phone and I could hear the social worker at the other end having a whispered conversation with somebody else.

'Well,' he said, 'he's burnt it down.'

'He's burnt what down?'

'He's burnt the school down,' he said, 'well, not the whole school, just the gymnasium but . . . well, other buildings caught fire and a lot of the children now need to be sent home.'

'Why?'

'Because they have nowhere to sleep.'

'Was anybody hurt?'

'No, as soon as he had done it he told them.'

'You mean as soon as he had set fire to it?'

'Yes . . . after a little while . . . after it had got going,' said my friend. 'Honest to God, Tom, you ought to see it, you wouldn't think a kid could do it.'

'I don't know,' I said. 'I've heard of this kind of thing, but it's the first time I've actually come across it. What's his name?'

'Dennis.'

'How old is he?'

'Eight . . . he is eight.'

'Eight.'

'Yes, he is a bright kid, you know, very intelligent.'

We agreed that the social worker should bring Dennis the following day. They were due to arrive at eleven o'clock in the morning and I waited with some interest for the arrival of the first arsonist I had ever encountered.

The morning wore on and I tended to forget about Dennis. It was Saturday and all the children were home from school. arrangements were being made for various groups to go out, some home for the week-end or out for the day with their parents. It was almost twelve-thirty by the time I had finished and got back to my office. Two minutes later a knock came on the door and I called for whoever it was to come in.

Dennis entered the room. Dennis would have got a part in any Huckleberry Finn film that Hollywood could have chosen to make. He so looked the part that I didn't really believe that this could be him. He just stood inside the door, a small carrier bag in one hand and a stuffed toy in the shape of a monkey tucked under his other arm. He was followed quickly by two social workers.

'This is Dennis,' said one of them. He was carrying a large suitcase and the other was carrying a teddy bear. I stood and looked at this little boy.

'Hello,' said Dennis.

'Hello.'

Dennis had bright ginger hair, wiry and unruly. He had a broad forehead and green eyes and it looked as if his nose had been put on his face as an afterthought – he wrinkled it as he talked. There were innumerable freckles across his nose and under his eyes. He had a wide humorous mouth and he stood looking at me quizzically with his head on one side.

'How many kids have you got here?' he asked.

'Fifty.'

'Am I the fiftieth or will I be fifty-one?'

'You are about forty-two.'

'But you said fifty.'

'Well, there are a few vacancies.'

'Not many kids getting into trouble?'

'Not all come here because they have been getting into trouble.'

'I have.'

'Have you?'

'Yes.'

'What have you been doing?'

'I have been down at a school,' he said.

'How long have you been there?'

'About two months.'

'Oh yes, and I take it you would prefer to be somewhere else?'

'Yes I would,' he said. 'I didn't like it down there at all.'

'Why not?'

'It's all fields and things.'

'Don't you like fields and things?'

'Not really.'

'Well, what about the school, wasn't that nice?'

'It wasn't bad, but I didn't like it.'

'Why not?'

'Well, because I didn't want to go there, did I?'

'I don't know,' I said. 'Why not?'

'Well, I didn't want to go there, I didn't know anybody there

11

so I didn't want to go, and then I didn't like it much.'

'For other reasons?'

'Yes.'

'For what other reasons?'

'Well, it was a bit posh, you know.'

'Was it?'

I noticed he was wearing a grey blazer and grey trousers. One of the social workers said, 'Here's your cap,' and handed him a bright red one with a yellow ring round it.

'You look very smart,' I said.

'Yes, I know, but I don't like the hat.'

'Don't you, why not?'

'Well, it's red.'

'You don't like red?'

'No.'

'Why don't you like red?'

'I've got red hair.'

'Don't you like that?'

'No.'

'Why not?'

'They call you names.'

'Who do?'

'The kids do, they call you Ginger and things.'

'And don't you like being called Ginger?'

'No. One of the teachers used to call me Carrots.'

'Well, he probably meant it nicely.'

'I know, but how would you like to be called Carrots?'

I said I really didn't know, I had never had it happen to me.

'Well, if you had, you would know what I mean,' said Dennis. He paused and looked round the office. 'Is this your office?'

'Yes, well mine and Mrs Hart's,' I said.

'She work here?'

'Yes, she does.'

'Hm, down at the school the headmaster's wife, she worked there too.'

'Did she?'

'Didn't see her much, though.'

'No?'

'No, I don't think she did much.'

'What makes you think that?'

12

'Because I never saw her much.' He put his monkey down on a chair, very carefully.

'Where did you get that?'

'My mother gave it to me.'

'Oh, when?'

'A long time ago, when I was a kid.'

'You're not a kid anymore?'

'No.'

The truth was that it had been given to him a long time ago in another children's home and he would never be parted from his monkey. Wherever Dennis went, his monkey went. He took it with him to class and he took it with him to bed. He didn't play with it much, he would just sit it carefully on a chair or on a window-sill and ignore it, but when the class was over he would go and pick up his monkey and stick it under his arm and at night he would place it carefully in his bed.

'You have left the school, then?'

'Yes, had to.'

'Did you?'

'Yes. They said they were bringing me here, said I would like it here.'

'Did they?'

'Yes.'

'Why did they say you would like it here?'

'They said I could always . . .' he picked the monkey up from the chair . . . 'I could always have him with me.'

'That's true. Couldn't you at the school?'

'No, I had to leave him behind when I went to class and things.'

'And you didn't like leaving him?'

'No.'

'Do you talk to him?'

'No, he can't hear me, can he?'

'No, I suppose not, just thought you might find him someone to talk to.'

'No, anyway I have left the school now and that's it. You see, they made me come away.'

'Oh, did they?' I said. 'Why was that?'

'I didn't like it.'

'You told me that, but why did you leave?'

'I burnt it down, well, not all of it.'

13

'Oh, on purpose?'

He placed both his arms on the top of my desk and put his head on his hands. 'Yes. Yes, I did.'

'You mean you thought it out and planned it?'

'Yes.' He changed the conversation abruptly. 'What do the kids do here on a Saturday?'

'Some go out to play football, some of the older ones go to watch Fulham and some go down to the cinema.'

'I like the cinema,' he said. 'Do you take them?'

'Yes, somebody would go with you, that's if you have enough pocket-money.'

'Do you use your pocket-money to go to the cinema?'

'Yes, you use part of it.' I looked at him. 'Yes, if you have pocket-money you could go,' I said, 'or haven't you got any?'

'No.'

'Have you had it this week?'

'Yes.'

'And you spent it?'

He nodded his head.

'What did you spend it on?' I asked innocently.

'On bloody paraffin, didn't I, of course.'

Ask a silly question and you get a silly answer.

2 MICHAEL

Another day, another child.

The social worker said over the phone, 'Michael, he is a delightful little boy, Tom; if you take him I am sure you will be able to help.'

'What makes you think that?'

I was always a little suspicious when social workers said, 'We know you are the only person who could be of help to this little boy.' It usually meant that everybody else had been tried and had said, 'No.'

'He has been in a foster home for the past eighteen months and the foster parents have asked for him to be removed.'

'Why?'

'He is a disturbed little boy and they just couldn't cope with him any longer.'

'What has been going on, what has been his problem?'

'It's difficult to say, the foster parents just say he rejects them.'

'How does he do that?'

'Well, I don't think he is very affectionate towards them and he often has temper tantrums; they don't appear to be able to control him at these times. We thought that if we brought him along you could have a look at him . . . and the psychiatrists and people . . . we need to be very careful when we place him the next time.'

'How many places has he been in?'

'He has been in two nurseries and this is the second foster home,

15

but in fairness the first foster home was only a temporary placement.'

'How long was he there?'

'Nine months.'

'Well, you had better bring him along.'

Michael was four, he came in followed by the inevitable suitcase and the few toys in a box. He stood holding the social worker's hand, his arm stretched up to reach her. I bent down to talk to him and he pressed himself against the social worker's leg.

'This is Mr Hart,' she said.

'Hello, Michael.'

He looked at me with those big eyes and solemn expression that all children have when they appear to be weighing up the adult. There was that kind of wary look in his eyes as if this little four-year-old was trying to put me in one of the categories of adults he had come into contact with in the past.

'Are you going to stay with us for a bit?'

The big solemn eyes moved from my face to the social worker's.

'You remember, Michael, I was telling you.'

Michael nodded. He let go of her hand and drew away from her leg then walked up the hall and stood looking into the fish tank. His expression never changed, he just looked solemnly and silently at the fish floating and swimming by his face. One of the housemothers came down. 'Hello, Michael,' she said. She looked at him and he at her; she was a very gentle and concerned young woman. Michael appeared to approve of her somewhat and he pointed at the fish tank.

'Yes, Michael,' she said. 'They all have different names. Do you know what they are?'

Michael shook his head. She proceeded to name some of the fish, then the three of us walked with Michael while he had a look at all that was going on. Some of the other children came over and spoke to him. When we got to the playroom he saw the big rocking-horse and turned to look at the social worker, and then, for the first time, he smiled. She picked him up and took him over to sit him on it. He rocked backwards and forwards and then he laughed out loud. The social worker was obviously very fond of Michael and, as I subsequently learned, he of her. Even now, after twenty years, they are still friends.

Michael gradually settled in. He was an inquisitive little boy

16

who was always doing something, always playing or climbing, and he was also a very likeable little boy; he was not fractious and he didn't fight with the other children.

He became somewhat of a favourite among the older boys and girls because he was such a pleasant, likeable child. He was seen by the psychologist, who said he was a boy of superior intelligence. He was seen by the psychiatrist. As far as we could tell he was an orphan; his parents' whereabouts were unknown. He had simply been left in the casualty department of a hospital when he was perhaps two months old and had been received into care. His parents were never found.

I got to know Michael very well. He would come running down the hall to be picked up and he would often push on the door of my office until he got it open; it had a self-closing spring to conform with fire regulations. He would always manage to get through before I could get to the door to open it. He would come and stand in front of the desk and I would say, 'Have you come to visit?' or, 'Are you going to stay awhile?' and he would run back to the door and stand waiting for me to open it, then off he would go. On other occasions he would walk round my desk and sit underneath it and sometimes have a sleep there.

The psychiatrist was concerned because she couldn't understand why he had come to us. He was said to be severely maladjusted, but as far as we could make out he seemed a very well-adjusted child at that time. He was said to be unaffectionate, yet he loved to be picked up and was very affectionate in return. He was the one little boy who always seemed to be enjoying himself. There must be something wrong.

A staff meeting was held at which various theories were put forward about Michael's problems. He must have problems, because everybody said he had . . . his foster parents had asked for him to be removed, he had been in two nurseries, in one he had been a very naughty and angry child, it was said. That was when he was two, or perhaps one and a half. He had temper tantrums, he cried at night and wasn't toilet trained until well after the usual time allowed for these things to happen. He would go into the play-yard and, like many children of his age, when he ran he would often come a 'cropper', but unlike the majority of children, who would just cry a little, Michael would cry bitterly until someone made a real fuss of him.

17

'He is not institutionalized in any way,' was one learned theory put forward at the meeting. 'He is capable of making relationships,' said another. There were various theories as to why he had settled down – perhaps it was a honeymoon period; perhaps if he was with us for, say, another three or four months, his behaviour would begin to show through. The psychiatrist said that as far as she could make out, if he were maladjusted, the rest of us were in a terrible state psychiatrically.

'What are we going to do with him?'

'Such a normal little boy ought to be in a foster home.'

The meeting adjourned without anything very conclusive being decided. The general feeling among the staff was that, in some way or other, Michael was not being very fair to us . . . after all, if he was maladjusted, at least he should let us know about it. He was making it difficult: we were supposed to be the ones who knew about those things, who made the assessments, and covering up at four was not really playing the game. And so the days went by . . . Michael alongside the others standing out as even more well-adjusted. As the weeks went by, the more settled he became and the happier he appeared to be.

It was summer-time and the children used to go in two or three carloads over to Richmond Park . . . the young children, that is. A hamper would be packed with sandwiches and drinks, and the children would be taken over to the park about ten in the morning and not picked up until evening. The kids enjoyed it, and so did the staff. But while getting ready to go out one day a house-mother came dashing down the corridor, banged on the office door and came in. 'It's Michael,' she said. 'It's Michael, it's all coming out. He is beginning to show all the things which have been said about him and which we haven't ever seen. Can you come?'

I followed her down the corridor into the boys' lavatories. In the middle of the floor stood Michael. His face was scarlet and a throbbing vein stood out on his forehead, tears poured down his cheeks and he stamped his feet one after the other in the middle of the floor. He was screaming at the top of his voice and his fists were clenched, beating the air.

'T'arnt out! . . . t'arnt out!' he kept shouting.

People were trying to calm him without much success. 'Please, Michael,' one of the housemothers was nearly in tears, seeing the boy's obvious anger and distress and his red, distorted face.

'T'arnt out! T'arnt out!' he kept shouting.

No amount of reasoning was of any use, and in the end I spoke rather sharply. 'Stop it, Michael, stop it at once.' Michael stopped, his feet still. The perspiration poured down his face, tears down his cheeks, and his clenched fists were pushed up to his eyes.

'Now,' I said, 'tell me what is the matter.'

Michael dropped his fists from his eyes and stared up at me. 'I can't tet it out, Mr Hart,' he said. 'I can't tet it out.'

We all looked at Michael and as he stood there he wet his trousers.

'Oh, poor little boy,' said one of the staff. Just another sign, everybody said without actually speaking, just another sign of his disturbance. The housemother took off his wet trousers and then he pointed to himself. 'I can't tet it out,' he said and it was then we discovered that he had his underpants on back to front and it was true . . . he couldn't get it out.

That was the only sign of maladjustment we ever saw in Michael; he was seen regularly by the psychiatrist, but to no avail, however hard we tried it was impossible to make Michael maladjusted. Our psychiatrist, as well as being a very human and compassionate person, also had a great sense of humour. In her psychiatric report she wrote, 'In conclusion, I can only suggest that whoever has the future care of Michael should always ensure that his underpants are put on correctly or has an emergency slit made in the back.'

As far as I know, Michael never required a diagnostic assessment again. And as far as I know, he lived happily ever after.

3 LIONEL

Lionel came to me for the summer holidays at a time when I was working in a large children's home. He and another boy were in a home for children of subnormal intelligence, when it had to close down temporarily owing to illness among the staff. With the summer holidays about to begin, these children had been spread around various children's homes.

Lionel and his friend were placed in my house. He was a tall, slim boy who came dressed in a grey jersey, the style of which went out in the late 1930s. It had a little woollen tie on it. He wore a pair of khaki shorts which came down below his knees, had boots on his feet which made them look extremely large and wore a pair of grey stockings – the gap between the tops of his stockings and the bottoms of his shorts was about two inches. His arms appeared long and his hands very large. He was a very simple boy and was no trouble, though he never held a conversation with anyone. His hair stuck up and no amount of water or the occasional dab of Brylcreem managed to keep it in place.

The other boys in the house thought he was something of an oddity and one lad asked him rather cruelly, 'Why don't you wear proper clothes?' but Lionel didn't seem to take offence. The only time he showed any great animation was at meal-times when he would eat carefully and slowly, but would go on eating as long as food was put in front of him. At first it was difficult to tell when Lionel had had enough.

21

When the other boys were playing he would just stand and watch. He was about thirteen years old, but much taller than the other lads in the house. They would invite him to join in their games. He didn't appear to have much idea of how to play football or cricket, but he would run after the ball and kick it, never in the same direction twice. They tried him in goal, but he had little idea of what he was supposed to do there.

The boys appeared to appreciate Lionel's handicap and took a protective interest in him. Each week there was a cinema show in the gymnasium or the school hall, and they would take Lionel by the hand – he seemed to enjoy every film. When there were horses or other animals in the film he would get very excited and bounce up and down in his chair; this would produce a howl of protest from the boys behind who said he was obstructing their view. There would be shouts of 'Sit down!' or occasional threats that someone would thump him. On one occasion, a boy as big as Lionel decided to thump him. He had been lecturing Lionel for a long time about sitting still when the film was on, but as Lionel seemed to take little notice of what he was saying, he hit him. Lionel promptly turned round and thumped him so hard he knocked him to the floor. After that, his punching power was much appreciated, and whenever he came in for criticism it was verbal – nobody threatened to punch him again.

The boys in our house began to take quite a pride in Lionel. They took him everywhere and introduced him to all and sundry. 'This is Lionel, the new kid in our house, big isn't he? Don't pick a fight with him because you know what he did to big Albert.' Although he didn't seem to be aware of it, Lionel had gained for himself a certain amount of prestige.

One day Paul came to see me. Paul was a little boy of Indian extraction who would wrap a towel round his head at bathtime to look like the part he was playing. He was always either an Indian prince, or Gunga Din, or he would sit cross-legged on the floor with a towel rolled up in front of him showing the others how snake charmers worked in India. The boy had never been in India, but this didn't inhibit him from explaining to the others how it was done. He was also a great practical joker, always having the other boys doing things and making them look slightly ridiculous, but it was done without malice, and since he was so popular, none of them ever took offence. One April Fool's day he had me go to the headmaster's office and knock on the door saying, 'I believe you sent for me, sir,' only to be told that it was 1 April and I was the fourth person to be sent there that day by Paul. Would I kindly tell Paul that, if he did it again, he would be sending for Paul himself and the consequences might be painful.

Paul came to me and said, 'You know that new kid, Lionel?'

'Yes,' I said.

'He never seems to laugh much except when the films are on and there are dogs and things.'

'No, he doesn't, he is rather solemn.'

'Does he go to one of those special schools?'

'Why do you ask?'

'I don't think he's daft, you know.'

'What makes you say that?'

'Well, he just follows you about and does what you tell him.'

'Oh.'

'But he is very funny.'

'In what way?'

'Well, you know those metal bottle-tops we had on the pop bottles on Saturday?'

'Yes.'

'He swallowed a handful.'

'HE DID WHAT?'

'He eats bottle-tops, sir.'

I looked at Paul and he looked at me. He looked extremely serious and stared me straight in the eyes, just as he had done when he sent me to the headmaster's office or had the other boys dashing up the drive after telling them there was a fire engine trying to put out a fire at the Lodge. On that occasion he had all the members of the house down there looking for a non-existent fire engine, and then he hid on top of the lavatory until he felt the boys were no longer likely to try lynching him.

'Thank you very much, Paul,' I said.

'Oh well, I thought I'd better tell you,' he said and off he went. I sat and thought about this for a while, and although I knew I was being stupid and doing exactly what Paul wanted me to do, I thought I had better go and ask some of the others. I did it as casually as I could so as not to appear too stupid. It was almost bedtime and the boys were in the kitchen drinking their cocoa.

'Do you know what Paul told me?' I said.

'He'll tell you anyfink,' said one boy.

'You are right, John,' I said. 'He told me Lionel has been swallowing bottle-tops. You haven't seen him do that, have you?'

'No sir,' they said. 'One of these days he will say something and no one will take any notice. He'll cry "wolf" once too often.'

'What do you mean, I'll cry "wolf"?' asked Paul.

We explained it to him and they went up to bed. I gave Paul a lecture. I told him that when he said such things he could make life difficult for a boy and it created a great deal of worry when he said things that were not true.

'Sorry, sir,' he said, and went to bed.

The next day was a Saturday and he came to me again.

'Sir.'

'What is it now, Paul?'

'That new kid, Lionel?'

'What's he done this time?'

'He swallowed a knife, sir.'

'What kind of a knife?'

'One you use for your breakfast.'

'Oh,' I said, 'did he? Thank you.'

'Pleasure, sir.'

'One of these days, Paul, I'm going to get very cross with you.'

'Yes, sir. Sorry, sir,' and away he went.

It was after lunch that day that another boy came to me. John was an extremely serious and sensible lad, in some ways far too serious. He had no relatives and was completely on his own. No one ever visited John.

'Sir, can I have a word with you?'

'Yes.'

'Not here, in the sitting-room.'

I followed John through into the little sitting-room. 'What is it, John?'

'That new kid, sir.'

'Yes, what about him?'

'He did something rather funny, sir.'

'What did he do, John?'

'He swallowed a fork.'

I looked at him. 'Have you been talking to Paul?' I asked.

'No, sir.'

'Are you pulling my leg?' I looked at John and I realized that, among the many things John did, pulling legs was not one of them.

'No, sir.'

'When did he do it?'

'Out in the kitchen.'

I walked down to the kitchen to see Lionel there. 'Have you been swallowing things, Lionel?' I asked, but Lionel just said, 'Sir?' Indeed, in the whole four weeks he had been there the only words he had said to me were 'Sir' . . . 'Good night' . . . 'Wash' and 'Drink'.

I spoke to my wife. 'What do you think?'

'Well, Tom,' she said, 'I can't see John thinking that was very funny; he wouldn't play that kind of joke on you.'

I went down to the headmaster's office. Saturday afternoon was the day for the cinema, and he was collecting the films to take along to the school hall.

'Can I have a word with you, sir?'

'Yes, what is it?'

I told him about Paul.

'I wouldn't take much notice of what Paul tells you,' he said.

'Yes, but then John told me.'

'What do you think?' he asked.

'I don't know, John might be mistaken in what he thought he saw, but he wouldn't pull that kind of joke.'

'You had better take him to the hospital then.'

We got the local car-hire people and I took Lionel by the hand to be driven to the local hospital. As it was Saturday afternoon the hospital was pretty deserted; we went into the casualty department and sat there for a long time. Lionel appeared to be quite happy as he sat staring around and now and again pointed to things. I would say 'Yes,' or 'Very nice,' and poor Lionel would nod his head as if he agreed or understood.

'What can I do for you?' said a nurse who had come up.

'I would like someone to examine this boy,' I said.

'Why?'

'He has swallowed a knife and fork,' I said.

It is very difficult to tell how one plucks up the courage to explain in a hospital that someone has swallowed a knife and fork. She looked at me in total disbelief.

'A knife and fork?'

25

'Yes,' and as an afterthought I said, 'and someone said some bottle-tops as well.'

'Oh.'

She looked at the boy and then at me. 'Is the boy all right?' she asked.

'Well, he doesn't seem to be complaining of any pain,' I said.

'No, I don't mean that,' she said 'I mean . . .'

'Oh yes, he goes to a special school.'

She looked at me. 'Do you work there?'

I shook my head. 'He is with me at the children's home' (which she knew) 'for the holidays; people have been sick in his own home.'

'Oh.'

She went away and was gone for some time, then she returned with a young doctor who came over to me in quite a businesslike manner. He was rather brusque and abrupt and, with a note of disbelief in his voice, he said, 'Nurse tells me this boy has swallowed a knife and fork.'

I nodded my head.

'When?'

'Well, the knife yesterday and the fork today.'

'Why didn't you bring him yesterday?'

'Well, the boy who told me . . . I thought he was kidding me.'

He nodded. 'And then what happened?'

I told him that another boy who was much more reliable had come up with the information that the boy had swallowed a fork.

'But you don't know for certain?'

I shook my head. I was beginning to feel speechless, along with Lionel, and I was also beginning to feel extremely foolish and stupid.

'Well, it's Saturday afternoon,' the doctor informed me, as if telling me there was about to be an eclipse of the moon.

'I know,' I said. I looked at the doctor and wondered whether I had interrupted his watching of the local rugby match or whether there was something else I was depriving him of.

'I'm very sorry,' I found myself apologizing.

'I suppose we had better have an X-ray,' he said. 'Get me a form, nurse.'

She brought the form. 'X-ray stomach,' he wrote, and he used the word 'alleged', . . . 'alleged to have swallowed a knife and fork.'

'And bottle-tops,' I said.

I began to feel that the more I said he had swallowed, the more plausible my story might sound. If he hadn't swallowed anything, at least they might feel there had been some justification for my taking him there.

The doctor and the nurse disappeared. A quarter of an hour passed before they came to collect Lionel. He went along with the nurse quite happily, and though she talked away to him he didn't seem to take much notice. She went into her apron pocket and told him that if he was a good boy she would give him the sweet she held in her hand. Not knowing Lionel, she wasn't aware that it was absolutely fatal to offer him sweets. Lionel promptly took it and put it into his mouth, paper and all. She looked a trifle surprised, but paid no attention and took him through a swing door and out of my view.

So there was only me left in the waiting-room, though occasionally somebody was pushed through in a wheelchair. Now and again a nurse floated by and gave me one of those smiles as if to say 'All will be well' – the smile that is supposed to reassure you, but only makes you feel that the worst has happened.

Lionel was away for about forty minutes. He came back with the nurse and the doctor and the only way to describe their faces was to say that they had a look of stunned disbelief. In his hand the doctor carried an X-ray film held by a clip at the top.

'Mr Hart,' he said, and his voice half conveyed an apology for his previous attitude. He beckoned to me, and I followed him into a little room at the side of the main hall. He stuck the plate up against a viewing panel and switched on the light.

'Look,' he said, and I looked. There, plainly to be seen, was a knife and fork, two teaspoons and innumerable round flat objects. I looked at the doctor and tried to give him that look – as much as to say 'I told you so' – but I was having great difficulty in getting my jaw back up from my chest.

'We'll have to operate,' he said. 'He rattles.'

I looked at him. 'Rattles?'

'Yes, he rattles. You can hear him rattle.'

I took his word for it; personally I never heard it.

'Where is he now?' I asked.

27

'Out there.'

I walked back to find Lionel sitting quite happily on his chair. He looked up and saw me.

'You had better stay with him.'

About half an hour later an older doctor appeared. 'Let me have a look at this sword swallower,' he said.

I pointed to Lionel.

'Hello young fellow. You're quite an ostrich, aren't you?'

Lionel just looked at him.

'Doesn't he speak?'

'Not much,' I said. 'He's . . . he goes to a special school.'

The doctor looked, but passed no comment.

'Who is going to sign for the anaesthetic?'

In those days we were not, as staff, allowed to sign anaesthetic forms, and I told him so.

'Well, someone will have to sign it,' he said.

Lionel sat there, knife and fork, teaspoons and bottle-tops still inside him.

'Can it kill him – all that stuff in there?'

'Well, let's say it won't do him a lot of good,' said the doctor.

Phone calls were made to the headmaster of the home and permission was given for Lionel to have his operation. He was operated on later that evening. After about two weeks the time came for him to be discharged. Arrangements had been made for him to return to the house before going back to the home from which he came, and where there were people who knew more about caring for boys who swallowed knives and forks.

I went up to the ward and helped Lionel to dress. The nurses all came to say good-bye to him as he walked down the ward and out into the corridor. As we walked out we met the young doctor who had first seen him in the casualty department.

'You had better wait a minute,' he said. 'The consultant will want to see you.'

'Why? Hasn't he agreed to him being discharged?'

'Oh, yes. He has agreed to his discharge all right. He is just down the corridor, he won't be a minute.'

We sat on the two hard chairs outside the ward and along came the surgeon who had operated on him. I stood up, and so did Lionel. He looked at Lionel.

'Good-bye, young man.'

Lionel just looked at him.

'Thank you, doctor,' I said.

'Oh, that's all right, that's all right, young man. Just do me a bloody favour, will you?'

'If I can.'

'Keep him away from dustbin lids.'

Lionel went back to his home. I never heard from him or about him afterwards. I did later learn that this kind of behaviour has a name. It is called 'Pica'.

4 FREDDY

Freddy was nine. He was a tallish boy for his age. He had hair that was almost white and it was curly. He had the look of an angelic choirboy and he spoke with a soft quiet voice; he never got dirty and was always giving good advice to the other children around him. Freddy attended a school for maladjusted children. He had spent a good deal of his time away from the school and had the annoying habit of entering people's houses and, if possible, stealing money. He was a boy who was thoroughly disliked by the other children. He had such annoying habits as picking up their cup of tea in the morning and quietly pouring it into their cornflakes, and if this didn't bring about the desired result, which was somebody threatening to thump him, he would run screaming to the nearest staff member saying he was being attacked.

On occasions he would break something that belonged to him and would then accuse another child of having done so. None of these little idiosyncracies of Freddy's endeared him to the other children. 'They don't like me,' he would say and looked very pained at the suggestion that there might be some justification for their somewhat antagonistic attitude towards him.

Freddy had been going to the Child Guidance Clinic from about the age of four. He would talk to the other children about the various schools he had been in and the cruelty of the teachers, and of the homes he had been in and how he had been ill-treated there. One morning Freddy was in the dining-room and a four-year-old

31

was sitting there waiting for his breakfast. Freddy took hold of the little boy's porridge and his cup of tea and quite deliberately poured both over the child. The staff who were having breakfast with them called me over and I went to the little one, who was crying. He was taken away to be cleaned up and I said I would see Freddy after breakfast. He sat with rather a smug expression and began to eat his breakfast.

After breakfast I stood in the dining-room with my deputy. 'What was all that about?' I said to Freddy.

'All what about?'

'Pouring tea and porridge over the little boy.'

'I did it,' he said, 'because I am maladjusted.'

'You're what?' I asked.

'Maladjusted.'

'I don't know anything about being maladjusted, but if you do that again I'll probably spank your backside for you.'

Freddy looked at me in horror. 'You can't do that,' he said.

'Why not?'

'Because I've already said I'm maladjusted.'

'I don't know anything about this maladjusted business,' I said. 'Do you know anything about it, Mr Smith?'

Leo looked at me. 'No,' he said.

'Well, if you did . . .' said Freddy.

'If I did what?'

'Spank my bottom,' he said, 'I would tell my P.S.W.'

'Your what?'

'My P.S.W.'

'What's that?' I asked.

'My psychiatric social worker, at the school where I go.'

'Oh,' I said, 'and what would she do?'

'She'd tell . . . well she'd tell the therapist there and he wouldn't like it. He'd report you to County Hall and you'd be in trouble.'

'Would I, now?' I said.

'Yes, you would,' he said, 'because when you're maladjusted you mustn't be spanked, because it doesn't do you any good.'

'Oh,' I said. 'Do you know what can do you good?'

'Yes, but it takes a long time,' he said. 'My therapist said it would probably take years for it to happen.'

'Oh,' I said. 'Well, I don't know, but if you do that again to that little boy I shall be very cross indeed. Do you understand?'

Freddy looked at me. It was a look of utter disdain. 'Yes,' he said.

He walked to the door and looked at Mr Smith.

'Humph,' he said. 'Doesn't know what a P.S.W. is and doesn't know what maladjusted is. How ignorant can you get?'

With that, Freddy turned on his heel and with great dignity walked out of the room.

5 NIGEL

One of the clearest memories I have of the many children I have had the privilege of working with in my life – one of the clearest impressions is of Nigel.

I remember the day that the social worker came to see us about him.

'This is a little boy who will cause you a lot of trouble.'

'Why, what's the matter with him?' I asked.

'He is subnormal, been in a special nursery for subnormal children and they are now asking for him to be removed.'

'Why is that?'

'Because of his constant screaming and the fact that some of the young nurses who have been caring for him have become very disturbed by his behaviour.'

'What are you going to do with him if I take him?'

'I honestly don't know, maybe you could take him for a while and perhaps he could be looked at to find out if there is anything that can be done to help.'

The social worker was obviously deeply concerned and it was agreed that she would bring Nigel to us. She duly arrived with him. He was dressed in a kind of romper-suit. They stood in the office doorway and he looked around. He had bright blue eyes and his hair was white and I noticed that it had a sort of wave at the front. He walked into the office, this delightful-looking child, taking no notice of the social worker or my wife, or of me. He picked up a pencil-box belonging to one of the children and began to bang it on the desk, and when the social worker tried to take it off him he just hung on and made a peculiar kind of high-pitched whine, then he let go. Then he picked up an ash tray and began to bang that. Each time an object was taken from him and we tried to give him something which would cause less damage, Nigel made this noise. I had never heard a child make a noise like it before.

The housemother came and picked him up and he promptly hung on to her hair with all his strength. It was as much as we could do to get him to release her hair. She put him down and I held out my hand and he took hold of it without trying to break my fingers off and we walked out into the passage-way. We walked down into the children's playroom where there were rocking-horses, roundabouts and toys. There were also some big wooden bricks and it was towards these that he was attracted. He took hold of a brick and banged it and banged it again and again on the floor. He just sat banging the brick on the floor.

The social worker said, 'Nearly all the children at the nursery do that, they sit and bang things in between their legs on the floor.'

'How subnormal is he, has anybody any idea?' I asked.

'They say at County Hall that he is very subnormal.'

'He doesn't look it, does he?'

'No, he is a beautiful-looking child, isn't he?'

'His parents?'

'We don't know.'

'Brothers and sisters?'

'He hasn't got any.'

The housemother eventually took Nigel off and sorted out his clothing. It all seemed inappropriate. Later, when she went to dress him in clothing more suitable for a little boy, dungarees and a shirt, she came back and said, 'He is wearing a napkin.'

'What for?'

'I don't know. I suppose he isn't toilet-trained yet.'

At the meal table Nigel would put his hands in his food and spread it all over his face and hair. If you picked him up, he immediately scratched you or pulled your hair. If another child went near him to play, he bit him. When he was spoken to, he took no notice but would pick up a toy and bang it up and down on the floor, faster and faster making a louder and louder noise; he did this with a kind of controlled fury which was quite frightening to see. If the toy smashed he would sit there and bang his fists, rocking backwards and forwards, backwards and forwards, hitting his head on cupboards or walls without seeming to hurt himself as far as anyone could tell. Given a sweet, he would suck it while rocking from side to side, and as he rocked he would clench his fists and one hand would go up in the air while the other was hitting the floor.

The housemother in charge of the little nursery group we had would take the little boys and girls to the lavatory, Nigel among them. He didn't seem to mind, and after a few days she stopped using his pair of rubber pants and nappy. As the weeks went by, Nigel allowed himself to be fed and his hands no longer went into his food quite so much, but he would still sit and rock, faster and faster, backwards and forwards and from side to side. When he banged on a loose cupboard door, the noise he made became almost unbearable, but when the radio or record-player was on, he would just look at it and walk away.

Few children dared to go near him because of his aggressive behaviour, but on the few occasions when a child hit him back Nigel didn't seem to be provoked into retaliation. He would just sit, and if they hit him again he would lie on the floor and make the screaming sound, which seemed to penetrate the whole building. Nigel required one person to look after him all this time. In some ways, he was a very unrewarding little boy to care for since there was no response from him. It was no use scolding him because that had no effect. The only two words he ever said were, 'naughty boy,' and one appreciated that these were the only two words which had penetrated through to him in the four years of his life.

His voice was indistinct, he spoke in a rather flat, dull tone and you never saw him laugh. The little beds that the four-year-olds slept in were of no use to Nigel; his bedroom was on the third floor and he would get out and wander off around the building, and up and down the long linoleum-covered stone staircases, so we had to find a big cot for him. The only thing which seemed to hold his interest was being able to look out of the dormitory window – he shared a small dormitory with eleven other children – and he would stand in his cot looking out of the window and watching the buses and the people going by.

I was sitting in the office one evening when my wife came in. She stood looking rather thoughtfully out of the window.

'Tom,' she said, 'Nigel . . .'

'What about Nigel?'

'I'm not so sure that he is subnormal.' As she was saying it another member of staff had come in at the door and we both looked at my wife, rather startled.

'I went upstairs a little while ago,' she said, 'and he was standing at the end of his cot looking out of the window.'

'Yes?'

'I spoke to him,' she said. 'I said "Nigel", but he took no notice, then I spoke much louder, but he still took no notice, so I shouted, but he just carried on looking out of the window.'

'Yes?'

'Then I touched the end of his bed and he turned round, looking quite startled.'

'If he is subnormal he probably doesn't understand words,' I said.

'I think he does,' she said.

'Why?'

'He looked at me as if he were trying to understand what I was saying to him.'

She discussed this with the housemother who cared for Nigel, and each day they took him on one side and talked to him, telling him what certain objects were, 'doll . . . doll . . . doll . . .' they said in front of him, pointing to the doll. The housemother would cuddle it and Nigel would stand and stare at her. After a week of this, he suddenly one day picked up a doll from the playroom floor, put it in his arms and cuddled it. And then . . . he laughed. The housemother said she understood how people felt when a miracle had occurred.

We took Nigel to the medical officer and my wife explained her suspicions about deafness. The doctor said, 'Hold him,' and clapped his hands behind the boy . . . nothing. We got in touch with the local authority responsible for him and said that we suspected deafness, only to learn that this had been thoroughly tested and that there was no question of deafness. We discussed it again with the medical officer.

'You still think he is deaf, don't you?'

'Yes, I do,' said my wife.

'Then let's get him to the hospital and tell them of your suspicions.'

'Can we do that?'

'Yes, he has a lot of wax in his ears and I will write and query whether or not there should be further investigations.'

We took Nigel up to the hospital. He was, as I have said, a beautiful child, and the staff at the Ear, Nose and Throat Hospital looked at him and smiled, but they could get no response.

He was taken away for examination and eventually we were called in to see the consultant.

'There is nothing wrong with his ears,' he said. He had a file containing the social history and medical background, and was extremely patient as we told him about Nigel and my wife's concern that he might be deaf.

'What did the people say when he was classified as subnormal?'

'That his hearing had been fully tested and he was deemed to be subnormal.'

The doctor picked Nigel up from his chair and stood him up, looking at his face, his hands and his teeth. Nigel stood quietly while this was being done, and we all got the feeling that, at this moment in time, Nigel knew this man was his friend.

'I will admit him,' he said at last.

My wife looked at me.

'What's the matter, don't you want me to?'

'It's just that he seems to have been pushed around so much lately and he just seems to be getting to know us.'

'I know,' said the doctor, 'but it will only be for two or three days.'

The three days lengthened into ten. Somebody went in every day to see Nigel, and somehow, each day, he appeared to be waiting. On the tenth day when my wife and I went back to the hospital Nigel was standing by the doctor's side. I went over and picked him up and felt him arch his back as he looked at me; he stretched out his hands for my hair and instinctively I hunched my shoulders, but this time he just took hold of it, he didn't pull it. The doctor sat at the other side of his desk looking at us.

'You are right, Mrs Hart, he is deaf,' he said. 'But it is a peculiar high-tone deafness. He has some hearing and with a specially prescribed hearing-aid he should be able to hear and should be able to talk.'

39

'Why . . . how . . . do you think this has happened?'

'I don't know,' he replied. 'It is fortunate you were so perceptive.'

'It was an accident, really,' said my wife.

'Yes, the kind of accident that needs following up,' he said. 'I have written to the Medical Officer of Health to explain what has happened and we will do an I.Q. test, but it must be done a little at a time, can you bring him up every day?'

Nigel was taken up every day and his I.Q. was said to be 112, though this was probably an under-estimate, which it subsequently turned out to be. I received a letter, disapproving in tone, informing me that I should not have taken Nigel to the hospital and that there were proper channels for de-ascertaining subnormal children and that Nigel had been found to be subnormal by very competent people. I had the feeling that whoever wrote the letter was saying, 'You have been very lucky this time, but . . . don't do it again.' The important thing was that Nigel was no longer to be considered subnormal, a hearing-aid was provided for him and he rapidly began to speak.

Nigel's behaviour, his rocking and the banging of his toys, was pure imitation of the other unfortunate children with whom he had found himself living, though perhaps some of the banging was a result of his own anger and frustration. The social worker was highly delighted, for she was fond of Nigel. We agreed to keep him for a time and he rapidly grew into a normal little boy, his conversation increasing and his desire for affection unbounded. He was equally capable of giving affection to those around him. His affection for the young housemother who had cared for him since the day he came to the home knew no limits.

The social worker, who had been systematically delving into Nigel's past, came to see us one day. 'I have discovered something which is going to shock you,' she said. 'I know it shocked me.'

'What is that?'

'Nigel has a sister.'

'How did you learn that?'

'I checked back until I found the date of his admission into care and I discovered that two children had been admitted on that day. One was admitted as Nigel 'A' and the other was a girl with a slightly different surname. The names had been spelt differently on the admission forms, but the second one was his sister.'

'And?'

'Well, they were separated; his sister is older than he is and they just haven't met up since.'

'How long has he been in care?'

'Since he was four months old.'

I could see Nigel playing in the yard, being pulled around on a truck by his housemother. He sat there, laughing.

Eventually a place was found for Nigel in a school for the deaf and he was reunited with his sister. He joined her in a foster home she had been in from almost the day after she had been admitted to care. Nigel stayed there, and at the age of eleven he went to a grammar school. He is today a very happy, intelligent and well-educated young man.

It was some years afterwards that I first visited a hospital for subnormal children. I walked round wards where there were hydrocephalic children, and wards where there were children just lying in bed not taking any interest in anything around them They were fed and kept clean. Then I came to a ward where two children were sitting on the floor with blocks of wood in their hands and they were picking them up and banging them down between their legs. Another child came over to them with a toy in his hand and hit one of the others with it. We stood and watched these children. I sat in the car going home, thinking about these children . . .

'Are you thinking about the children banging the bricks?' asked my wife.

I nodded my head.

'Did it disturb you?'

'Yes.'

'You were thinking of Nigel?'

'Yes, I wonder how many Nigels there are in the world,' I said.

'I shouldn't think there are very many.'

I looked at her, and to this day I am not sure, but I think like me she was wondering if there was just one . . . It is a disturbing thought, and every time I pass a hospital where such children live, I think of Nigel and, for some reason, feel genuinely afraid.

6 GARY

Gary arrived and entered our lives, for a little time creating more problems than one could reasonably expect a child of seven to create. He was a fat little boy who looked like an infantile Fred Emney, and always carried with him a little brown leather vanity case. The first time I saw him with it I asked, 'What have you got there, Gary?'

Gary lisped, and in his lisping voice he said, 'In thith bag I have two toilet rollth, a blue one and a yellow one, and they are mine and I don't let anybody elth uthe them.'

'Oh,' I said.

'Would you like to look at my toilet rollth?'

I said I would be very honoured to be given this privilege. He opened up the bag and, sure enough, there were two toilet rolls.

'Have you any other treasures?' I asked.

'Yeth, I have.'

'What other treasures have you got?'

'I will show you,' and he departed to his locker. In there he had two more toilet rolls.

'I suppose they are your spares, are they?' I asked.

'Yeth,' he said, 'I like toilet rollth.'

Apparently in the lavatories he was always quite content with the paper provided by our local councillors and ratepayers. His own toilet rolls, as far as one could make out, were a kind of status symbol. Nobody else except Gary collected toilet rolls and nobody I have met before or since could produce them with such a flourish to be shown as works of art. Gary was well before his time. It was years later that the artistic *avant garde* latched on to Gary's theory and made fortunes for themselves. Gary was unfortunately also epileptic and he would have a fit about once a week, or sometimes three in a fortnight, and after each of these occasions, like all children who are epileptic, he would sleep deeply. Immediately on waking he would walk on unsteady legs to look for his vanity case and his toilet rolls.

He was a very affectionate little boy.

'I love you, mith,' he would say in his lisping voice.

'I love you too, Gary.'

'Yeth, mith, I knew you would,' he would say.

He would go and sit in the middle of the playroom with the other children and look around until he saw some child on his own, then he would go, complete with his case, and pull up a little chair and sit down opposite the other child with his nose practically against the latter's nose.

'Whath your name?' he would say.

The other child would tell him, 'My name is John,' or whatever it might be.

'Do you like it here, John?' Gary would ask.

John would say yes or no, depending on his mood or his degree of honesty.

'I like it here. Would you like to look at my toilet rollth?'

It was a question which always produced a 'yes', from children because they were normally polite, and from adults out of a sense of curiosity.

Christmas was about a month away. 'What do you want for Christmas?' Gary was asked by an over-enthusiastic visitor.

'I want two toilet rollth and thum thothage and math.'

'Sausage and mash, what do you want that for? Wouldn't you like turkey or chicken and plum pudding?'

'No.'

'Why not?'

'Becauth I like thothage and math, and all the otherth can have the plum pudding and turkey.'

'Don't you like it?'

'Thothage and math?'

'No, plum pudding.'

44

'I've had it,' said Gary.

'Well, haven't you had sausage and mash before?'

'Yeth.'

'Well, why do you want sausage and mash?'

'Becauth I can remember what thothage and math tatht like,' he said, 'and I liked it.'

Perhaps turkey coming round once a year wasn't something that stuck in his memory.

Gary also had a habit of wandering when he was getting ready for a bath at night, or when he had got out of the bath and had dried himself and was waiting for a member of staff to sort out his pyjamas. His rather fat little towelled figure, complete with vanity case, walking down the hallway was a sight that really had to be seen to be believed. Visitors in the front hall, social workers and mothers of children would be amazed to see Gary walking up carrying his case. He would stand and look at them quite solemnly, put down his case then stare up at them. 'Whath your name?' Visitors would always answer him.

'I've juth had a bath,' he would say.

'Oh,' they would say, 'and are you going somewhere to get your pyjamas?'

'No,' he would say, 'I don't wear pyjamas.'

'Oh.'

'Would you like to look at my toilet rollth?' and he would open up his case and show them his toilet rolls. Whereupon this obese little figure would turn round and march off in the direction from whence it came. Whenever Gary had been on one of these journeys, he always managed to reduce his audience to a sense of absolute quiet, leaving them with a feeling of awe and wonder. There was always an overwhelming desire to laugh, and yet he was so solemn and so intense in his manner that to do so would have been doing more than offending him, it would have been downright rude.

As Christmas grew nearer we had visits from committee members and others who came to ensure that the home was being run reasonably efficiently and with due concern for the children.

I was going round late one evening with a committee member who had come with her two children, who had wandered off leaving me to show her around. She was a delightful person with a good sense of humour and very interested in the children's welfare as well as that of the staff of the home. As we began to

45

walk around another committee member arrived. She was rather an intense lady, but also one who was very concerned. But she had read the Curtis Report and was inclined to be suspicious of the way children were treated in children's homes. So she joined us, and as we began our tour of inspection we met Gary at the bottom of the stairs leading to his dormitory. He was in his pyjamas this time. He stood on the stairs, looking at the three of us.

'Hello, little boy,' said the first lady.

'What's your name?' said the second.

'Gary.'

'And what have you got in your case, Gary?'

'My toilet rollth,' he said.

The lady looked from Gary to me and back to the first lady. 'Toilet rolls?'

'Yeth,' he said. 'A blue one and a yellow one.'

'What does he want toilet rolls for?'

'Well, he likes them,' I said, 'he . . .'

'Oh.'

'Do you like it here?' asked the second lady.

'No,' said Gary.

'Why not?'

'Becauth they beat you.'

I could feel the cold shivers go down my spine as I gazed helpless at this tubby little figure ruining my image and good name. Any thoughts of advancement that I might have had in the service of children seemed about to be reduced to ruin out of the mouth of this little fat boy.

'Beat you?' said the second lady.

'Yeth.'

'Who beats you?'

'Mr Hart beath you,' said Gary, and he looked at me through half-closed eyes.

I looked back at her, by this time feeling quite sick.

'How does he beat you?' she asked.

'With a thtick,' said Gary, 'a big thtick, a long one.'

'With a stick, when?'

'Every day . . . nearly,' said Gary.

'Where does he beat you?'

'On my bottom.

'Yeth,' said Gary. 'He beath me and he beath me and my

bottom is covered all over with blood,' he said.

By this time I had an understandable urge to sink slowly through the floor.

'Till blood comes all over your bottom?' said the lady.

'Yeth, you thee he hath a thtick and it hath a nail in it.'

That nail was my salvation. I looked at the first lady, who looked at me, then at the second lady and back to Gary. Suddenly the first lady began to laugh, while I made a sickly attempt to smile, though at that moment my inclination was to open up Gary's little case, remove his toilet rolls and shove their owner inside instead.

My wife arrived and went off with the second lady while I took the first one to look for her children. We walked on talking to the children until we reached the bathroom. Sitting on a chair in his pyjamas was Gary, and in the bath, with no clothes on at all, were the committee lady's children. My mortification was complete. I looked at her and she at me, and again she burst into laughter.

'What are you doing there?' she asked one of her own.

'The lady said "Come on, hop in" so we did,' he said.

I turned to the housemother.

'Good God,' she said, 'I thought they were new children from the group next door.'

The children got dressed and the lady laughed again and said that she had never known them so willing to get ready for bed.

Shortly afterwards her husband became a Cabinet Minister, but I was never reported to the Privy Council. Gary went his way eventually to a children's home, complete with vanity case and toilet rolls. He had asked for sausage and mash for Christmas, and his housemother had seen that he got it.

7 TRADITION

A song sung by the children in the first children's home I went to work in went as follows, sung to the old revivalist hymn tune, 'There is a Happy Land':

> There is a mouldy dump, down Wandsworth way,
> Where we get knocked about, sixty times a day.
> Eggs and bacon we don't see,
> We get sawdust for our tea,
> That's why we're gradually
> Fading away.

They used to sing it to the staff with great gusto, more in fun than in protest. I have heard many variations of this song in different parts of the country since then, in children's homes and approved schools.

It's a kind of 'Eton Boating Song' for deprived children.

8 JEAN

Jean was seven years old. She came walking down the passage the day she was admitted, holdng the hand of her three-year-old brother.

'Hello,' she said.

'Hello. Are you Jean?'

She nodded. 'This is Patrick.'

'Hello, Patrick.'

Patrick looked at me wide-eyed and moved closer to his sister. 'There's no need to worry,' she said. 'The gentleman won't hurt you, will you?'

'No, I won't hurt him.'

'Of course not,' she said. 'I was just going to show him where he'll be sleeping.'

'How do you know?'

'The lady showed me, the one the girls call "Auntie".'

'Oh. Well, you'd better go then.'

'What do they call you?'

I told her. She walked up the stairs with the little boy, speaking to him in a way I've heard many mothers speaking to their children.

As she settled, she gradually allowed others to do more for her brother. She was a strange and sad little girl in some ways, she had such an adult manner and could care for the little boy as efficiently as any adult in the place, dressing him and bathing him and making sure he went to the lavatory.

'You take great care of Patrick,' I said to her one night. I was sitting in an old chair in what was the children's sitting-room.

'Yes. I take care of him,' she said, 'I took care of my mummy too.'

'How did you do that?'

'Well, when my mummy was ill I used to take care of her. She's in hospital now, you know.'

'Yes,' I said, 'I know.'

'I put my daddy in the police station.'

'Yes.'

'My mummy had a baby.'

'Yes, I know.'

'My daddy didn't want my mummy to have a baby,' she said, 'not another. He said there were enough with us, me and Patrick.'

'Did he?'

'Yes. One day he hit my mummy and knocked her down the stairs.'

'What did you do?'

'I hid behind the door till he'd gone. Patrick, well . . .'

'What about Patrick?'

'I locked him in a cupboard because I knew . . . well, I knew my daddy was angry. When he'd gone my mummy went to bed and then she tried to get some water and some towels . . .'

'Yes.'

'My mummy told me what to do and she had a baby.'

'She had a baby?'

'Yes,' she said. 'My mummy said afterwards I was better than the nurse.'

'What did you do?'

'I got a policeman.'

'And then what?'

'I took him back with me and well, he saw my mummy . . . and I'd washed the baby. Mummy had wrapped him in a towel.'

'And then what happened?'

'Well, they got an ambulance and they got my mummy and they took her away, then they brought me and Patrick here. I know they went and got my daddy because Miss told me.' ('Miss' was her social worker.)

Her story was true, every word of it.

Jean was enuretic. She started talking one day to the psychiatrist who was with us at that time. He was standing in the doorway of the office as she went by.

'Hello, Jean.'

'Hello, doctor.'

He picked her up and sat her on the shelf of the hatch that went through to the kitchen from the corridor. 'How are you?' he asked.

'I'm very well, thank you. You know, doctor, I have a nice dream.

He didn't prompt her but just nodded his head.

'I have this nice dream, and when I dream, I dream I'm with my mummy and we go to the shops and she buys us nice things, Patrick and me, then she goes away.' She put her head on one side and looked at him. 'And then I wet the bed.'

'Do you know you're wetting the bed?'

'Yes, but I'm not awake,' she said.

'No, I know you're not.'

'And it's all warm and I feel, I feel ever so good, just as if my mummy was nursing me, but when I wake up in the morning, it's all cold and sticky.'

'Thank you for telling me, Jean,' he said.

'That's all right.'

He lifted her down from the shelf.

''Bye, doctor.'

''Bye, Jean.'

Jean and Patrick did go back to their mother. Patrick loved Jean and their mother loved both of them, but I have never met a child with so much love and so much concern within her as Jean. She went home and I never heard of her again, but she was a remarkable, a remarkable lady.

9 AMANDA

Amanda was brought in late one evening. She was carried in, wrapped in a blanket. She was nine years old. She was carried through into the office, but she didn't stand up when the blanket was taken off her and she was put down on the floor; she sank to the floor and crawled. She made a peculiar noise as if singing to herself. She was dirty, she was not verminous, but the dirt was grimed into her and she smelled of stale urine and faeces. When I picked her up she went rigid in my arms, then limp, totally limp, so that I had to hold her or she would have slipped on to the floor. I carried her upstairs to a bathroom and the staff undressed her and put her in the bath. At first she resisted entering the water, but when she got in it she splashed her hands on the top of it very much as babies do. She was washed and had her hair washed and she was put into a nightdress, but again she crawled. When anyone went near her, she cringed away as if expecting to be hit.

'What's happened to her?' asked one of the staff.

'She's been locked in a room for five years,' I said.

'Oh my God, what for?'

'No one really knows yet, except that the family thought she was subnormal and, well, they were ashamed of her.'

Amanda was cared for, and again I was amazed at how quickly she responded. She was soon walking. It looked as if Amanda could understand all that was being said to her, but it was some weeks before she began to talk. Her family were quite well-to-do, hcr two brothers went to a boarding-school, and her father was a wealthy and successful man. The daughter was, in a sense, her mother's shame. She had thought that the girl was ugly and defective.

Amanda was actually a rather pretty, dark child with her dark hair, dark complexion and deep brown eyes. She responded to kindness and interest and was obviously bright. She was quick to imitate what girls of her own age did, she was soon able to join in their games and would watch all that they were doing so that she could join in the next time. She quickly learned to eat her meals with a knife and fork and not with a spoon as she had done at first; sometimes she had just picked up the plate and eaten from that. She very quickly learned to go to the lavatory, and although she was enuretic for some months, this also cleared up in due course.

There was some talk of prosecuting the parents, but the other two children proved to be loved and well cared for. The parents were fond, affectionate parents and the decision was made not to prosecute them. The man's livelihood would have been taken away, a good loving home for the sons would have been broken up – as would what was, on the surface, a reasonable marriage. Would it have made things any better for Amanda? Or erased what had happened to her during the past five years?

The father visited, and I looked at this man as he stood in the hall. He was a handsome man and there was a boy with him.

'Wait in the car,' he said to the boy.

'No, I would like to see her,' said the boy.

'Can I see you for a minute?' the man asked.

I nodded and went into the office as he followed.

'I suppose you are wondering what kind of a man I am,' he said.

I said the thought had crossed my mind.

'And I suppose you think I am unfeeling and uncaring?'

'Those are your words,' I said. 'You are the one who obviously needs to say them.'

He nodded. 'I suppose you are wondering why.'

'I must say I wondered how you could let it happen.'

'I love my wife,' he said, 'and she is a good mother to the boys and a good wife to me, but . . .'

'But Amanda,' I said.

'She just felt that she was ugly and . . . well, defective.'

'Why didn't you make some other arrangements if you had to?'
I asked. 'You aren't without money?'

'She was so ashamed, she had such a fear that people would
know about her.'

'Well, they must have done.'

'You see, we bought a bigger house so that Amanda could have
a room of her own.'

'But the room . . .' I said. 'The bed was soaked in urine and the
linoleum and the french windows were washed down rather like
you do for an animal.'

The man nodded.

'But she is your daughter as well, isn't she?'

'Oh yes, she is my daughter. I tried to persuade my wife to do
other things and I thought that gradually she would, but time
goes by and, in a way, Amanda didn't seem to be part of the home
any more.'

'Didn't you ever go in and talk to her?'

'Not much.'

'What about the boys?'

'Mother told them that they mustn't mention her, and when
they were at home she would cover up the french windows so that
they couldn't see in.'

'Would she be in the dark?'

'No, we put the light on.'

'Who put her to bed?'

'I did occasionally.'

'Who bathed her?'

'I did now and again.'

I sat looking at the man as we sat there. I was about thirty-two
and he must have been about forty. I had always imagined that
cruelty was something that was perpetrated by cruel people, but
this wasn't a cruel man.

'When you had friends visit the house or come to stay with you,
what then?'

'The room was a small one at the back of the house. It is a big
house.'

'It has french windows.'

'Yes, but that is not one of the main rooms, it goes out into the
back; I think it was an office at some time or another.'

'An office?'

57

'Yes, the man who lived there before I did used it as an office for his business.'

'So they never knew or went near?'

'No.'

'Didn't they ever hear her?'

'No, they wouldn't hear her there.'

'You have servants?'

'We have had two since before Amanda was born.'

'And what did they think?'

'Betty would go in and look at her now and again,' he said. 'They just thought she was simple-minded. We were looking after her the best way we could. The room was warm.'

'What about when you went on holiday?'

'Well, we just went and Betty would look after her.'

'What I still can't understand is why you let it happen.'

'As I said, my wife. Whenever she was mentioned my wife would . . . would shout, I suppose you would call it, become hysterical.'

'I suppose it was difficult when the boys were home.'

'Well, you know the effect it can have on children.'

'Didn't you ever think of the effect it was having on Amanda?'

'Not at first and, well, you grow used to it, you know.'

'But what about when she grew older, what would you have done then?'

The man stood up and put his hands on the top of the desk. 'Christ only knows. Some nights I would wake with a feeling of panic and go down to see if she was all right. I used to worry in case she died. God, what would we do if she died?'

'Your wife?'

'No. She never worried . . . it's funny, really, she really loves the boys.'

He sat for a while. 'Can I see her?'

'Yes.'

I took him through to the playroom where Amanda was, and at first he didn't recognize her. She was wearing a little cotton dress and someone had put ribbons in her hair which they had plaited because it was quite long. The housemother took her by the hand and brought her over and the man just stood and looked down at his daughter then turned and went out of the room, back up the passage towards the office. Amanda pulled away from the housemother and walked to the door to stare after him; she didn't say anything, but walked back to the housemother, looking puzzled and worried.

'What is the matter, Amanda?'

She just leaned against the housemother.

The man stood staring at the fish in the tank in the hall. 'She looked so different.'

His son came back through the front door. 'Have you seen her, dad?'

His father nodded.

'Can I see her?'

The father shook his head.

'I want to,' said the boy and walked down the passage and into the playroom. Then I saw him walking back up the passage with Amanda, who would not let go of the housemother's hand.

'I brought her, dad,' he said.

Near the front door was a flight of stairs and the man walked over and sat down on them. Amanda stood looking at him and he half held out his hands. Amanda, pulling the housemother with her, went over to him and he took her hand in his. The boy stood by the side of the stairs, looking at me. The father got up and, still holding the child's hand and with the housemother on the other side, walked out to the play-yard at the back of the house. The boy still stood there.

'You think it's terrible, don't you?'

I looked at the boy and nodded my head. 'Yes.'

'So do I, and my brother. So does he, really.'

'Who, your father?'

'Yes, my father. He tried to be good to her, we tried to be kind.'

'He wasn't very successful.'

'No. He couldn't be, really, my mother wouldn't let him. You don't really understand, sir.'

'I think maybe I do,' I said.

'Will they send anyone to prison or anything?' he said. 'Will people know?'

'No, I don't think so.'

'Will they find out how . . . ?'

'Will who find out, the neighbours?'

'No. How you . . . well, how you people found out.'

'No. By the way,' I said, 'how did they find out?'

59

The boy looked at me. 'I don't know,' he said, but we both knew. I found that I had held out my hand in a strange kind of way and thought I was going to put it on his shoulder then stopped half-way. The boy smiled and shook my hand. The father came back.

'We had better be going,' he said to the boy.

'Yes, dad.'

'Can I see you for another minute?'

We went back into the office.

'How did they find out about her?'

'You mean?'

'Somebody must have told you.'

'Yes.'

'But you don't know who?'

'No. It was an anonymous tip-off.'

'I wonder why they didn't phone the police,' he said.

'I don't know.'

The father looked at me for a moment. 'Are you sure you don't know?'

'Yes, I am sure.'

He smiled and said, 'I will come and see her again.'

'Do that.'

'You don't mind?'

'I have no reason to mind, you are her father.'

'I don't mean like that,' he said.

'No, you come.'

He half held out his hand then changed his mind and put it in his pocket and took out a wallet.

'Will she?'

'No, she doesn't need anything. You can give her half a crown or something as you go out, that will mean more to her than leaving something with me.'

Amanda stayed for about twelve months. She developed into a laughing, affectionate child, though at times she was very quiet and would sit on her own and appeared to have lost contact with us. Initially these were long periods, but they gradually lessened. Her I.Q. when tested was said to be about 80. She went to a boarding-school and during the next two years she was tested again and found to be of above average intelligence.

The father visited each week and the boys frequently came with him. Amanda would wait for them at the door with her housemother, and when they arrived she would stand patiently while they took her by the hand. Then came a time when she began to get quite excited, and when they arrived she would forget to kiss her housemother, for whom she had come to have a great deal of affection, and she would run towards her visitors and then run back. When her birthday came round her father bought her a bicycle which had every conceivable gadget imaginable on it.

Eventually a decision had to be made as to where Amanda should go. She was taken to see a school which cared for children who had disturbed backgrounds and who were retarded in learning, as she was. There she went, and she settled in quite happily. For some time she came back to us for the holidays and the father would come with the boys and take her out. But, in all that time, the mother never visited. Gradually Amanda was introduced to a family who lived near the school and went to stay with them during the holidays. The last time she stayed with us, the father came to see me before she went back.

'Does her mother never ask after her?' I asked.

'No.'

'And does she know you are visiting her?'

'Yes.'

'Does that make for difficulties?'

'No. In some way she convinces herself that it is not really happening. The boys have grown very fond of her, don't you think?'

'Yes. How about you?'

'Yes, you might not believe it but I love her too,' he said. 'Can you believe that?'

'Yes, I believe that.'

'Can you understand how it happened?'

'Yes, I can see how it happened, but in some way I can't understand how you let it happen, but yes, I know.'

'The first time I came to meet you . . . you have no idea how ashamed I was.'

'Yes, I have,' I said. 'Strangely enough, it was that which . . . well, which stopped me making judgements which perhaps were the wrong ones. What you did to that child was terrible.'

'I know,' he said. Then he spoke to the housemother who had cared for Amanda. 'I would like to thank you,' he said. 'I would like to give you something to show my appreciation.'

61

'I don't want anything,' she said.

He looked at her.

'No,' she said. 'Not for any other reason but that . . . well, you know, in this job you get a lot of brickbats thrown at you, but Amanda is part of my life now.'

He held out his hand and the housemother took it. I walked with him to the door. His big car was outside and his son got out and came over. 'Good-bye, Mr Hart, and thank you very much.'

'You have nothing to thank me for,' I said. 'It was a pleasure.'

But we both knew what he was talking about and as his father looked at me I knew that he knew too.

'I thought . . .' he said.

'What?'

'Nothing,' he said and held out his hand.

'Good-bye,' he said.

'Good-bye.'

I never saw him again, and I never saw Amanda again. I heard that she grew up into a person who was attractive, gentle, but very timid, and that her father, whom she grew to love, arranged for her to live abroad.

It is perhaps difficult to understand how anyone could gradually grow to have a great deal of sympathy for the father of this child. Yet he was a man with a lot of love to give to Amanda and his sons. His sons knew it but they had one advantage: they also knew their mother, and I never met her. As I said, perhaps he was a weak man but he was neither a wicked man nor a cruel one.

10 DISCRETION

Shortly after going to the first establishment of which I was ever in charge, I was standing in the front hall about eight o'clock one evening when the front door burst open violently and the biggest Irishman I'd seen for many years stood there. In a broad Irish accent he said, 'I'm looking for the boss. Where is he?'

I drew myself up to my full five feet nine inches and confronted this man with what I thought was dignity and charm and an air of conciliation.

'I am,' I said.

A hand as big as a mechanical shovel came out and grabbed me by the coat front and I seemed to go up and down in the air at an alarming rate before landing gently back on my feet.

'My son was here,' he said.

'When?' I asked.

'About three weeks ago.'

My desire to conciliate and impress the man with my dignity and charm evaporated and I fell back on one of my more natural assets, cowardice.

'That was before my time,' I said.

'Are you sure, now?'

'I'm sure.'

'Because if you're not,' he said, 'I'll put you in that bliddy fish tank.'

I looked at the fish tank, which was four foot six long, and appreciated that if he was going to carry out his threat he would have to break me in two. I also appreciated that he was a man who could do it. 'Come in to the office,' I said, 'and I'll see if I can be of service to you.'

I realized that I was being very servile but felt that this at least would ensure my health and safety. At that moment my wife appeared on the scene.

'Good evening,' she said charmingly to the man.

'Good evening ma'am,' he said. 'I've been talking to him,' pointing at me with his finger, 'but I don't appear to be getting anywhere.'

'I've been talking to him myself for ten years and I often feel a bit like that,' she said.

'Have you, now?'

'Yes,' she said. 'I'm Mrs Hart and he's Mr Hart and we've only just come to run this place.'

'Have you, now?'

'Yes.'

'Well, there's many things going on in this place that you ought to know about.'

'Such as what?'

'We'll go into your office, ma'am, if you don't mind,' he said looking up and down the corridor.

My wife led him into the office and I followed a close third.

'First,' he said, 'they're stealing off the children.'

'Who are?' asked my wife.

'All of them.'

'All of who?'

'All of them who were here before you came.'

'What have they stolen?'

'A pair of trousers I bought for my son and his rosary beads.'

'Well, I don't know about the trousers. Would you know them again?'

'They're brown corduroy.'

'Well, I don't know where they'd be, but I could give you a pair that would fit him, if that would do – a new pair.'

'That would be foine of you, ma'am,' he said. 'What about the rosary beads?'

'Would you know them again?'

'Sure I would,' he said. 'Didn't I buy 'em myself and give 'em to him?'

'Come with me then.'

I followed them both down the corridor and my wife led the way to a door on the right. On the table in the store-room were some new trousers that had been bought for the little ones.

'Would any of these fit him?'

'I'm sure they would, ma'am,' and he picked out a pair of corduroy ones. 'And his rosary beads, ma'am?'

My wife pulled back a curtain hanging at one of the windows and there, on three nails knocked into the window casing, were rosary beads of every shape, size, colour and description. Some were jumbled up and tied in knots and some just hung there, white ones and green ones.

The man looked at Barbara and then at me. 'Conspiracy to deprive the bliddy Catholics of their faith,' he said. 'Don't you think so, missus?'

'It certainly looks as if a number of them forgot to take them home with them,' she said. 'Would you know your son's amongst that lot?'

'No, I wouldn't. I really wouldn't.'

She took down the many rosary beads that hung there and went through them until she found a child's set that looked fairly new, though a little tangled.

'Do you think these would replace the ones your boy lost?'

'Yes. Thank you kindly, ma'am.'

'Would you like a couple of sets for yourself?' she asked.

'I wouldn't mind one,' he said. 'I'll have the Irish horn one over there.'

Not having much idea of what an Irish horn was, my wife untangled them and handed him the ones he pointed to.

'Would you be a Catholic yourself, ma'am?' he asked.

'No,' she replied. 'I wouldn't.'

'Huh, what would you be?'

'Well, that's difficult to say at the moment.'

'But I'm not thinking you'll be depriving the children of their rosary beads, will you?'

'I wouldn't dream of doing so,' said my wife, and went away to get a brown-paper bag to put the trousers in. The big man stood in the hall looking at the fish tank.

'Is your little boy at home?' she asked as she came back with the parcel.

'No missus, he isn't. He's in one of those children's homes, you know, they moved him from here.'

'Oh,' she said.

'His mither's dead, God rest her.'

'I'm sorry to hear that.'

'Yes, it was just that I'd bought them for him and I wanted him to have something I'd given him, you know.'

'I understand.'

He walked towards the door then came back and held out his hand to my wife. 'Thank you, missus,' he said.

'That's all right.'

He turned to me. 'Did I frighten you?' he asked.

I treated this with utter disdain. 'Certainly not.'

'Did I worry you?'

I looked at him.

'I usually do,' he said, 'worry 'em when I'm in a bit of a temper.'

'Yes, well,' I said, 'I admit you worried me a bit.'

'I tought I did, I tought I did,' he said. 'I'm sorry.'

He held out his hand and shook mine then walked out of the door. I walked out with him and stood on the kerb – this big man with the brown paper parcel in one hand and the rosary beads in the other. He sort of shook his hand until the rosary beads were in the middle of his palm, went to put them in his pocket, stopped, then lifted them up to his lips, put them in his pocket and walked off up the road.

I never did know who his child was. I had a feeling that his anger was not really about the trousers or the rosary beads at all, but I often think I was very lucky not to end up sharing a glass dish with the tropical fish.

INTERLUDE: THE OPPRESSED

I don't know how old I would be, perhaps ten or eleven, and I lived at that time during the years of the Great Depression between Oldham and Manchester. The big mills around Hollingwood had closed down. The Heron Mill was having its floors ripped out and sold for firewood, the machinery long since gone, some of it sold and transported to Japan. The Chamber Colliery in Hollings Road looked black and grim, and the men sat outside, their snack boxes between their legs and a bottle of water by their side. A majority of men took two slices of bread and lard to work; the lard didn't clog their mouths like cheese or jam, but they couldn't afford cheese or jam anyway. If there was work that day and they were called to the pit, then they would eat their bread and lard down below in seams not eighteen inches high. If not, they took it home to their children and wives.

The trams used to clang up and down between Hollingwood and Oldham, and some of them went as far as Failsworth and on into Manchester. The streets that led off the main road were narrow and grimy and there were little shops which had been there, and in the same family, perhaps for generations: shops where people could get a bit of tick, where tea could be bought by the ounce, where it was possible to buy a penny's worth of broken biscuits and where children would go in and ask if they had any stale teacakes. These could be had at two for a halfpenny. They were taken home and toasted, and didn't taste too bad. There was margarine of all brands which looked deep yellow, buttercup yellow, and had the texture of axle-grease. In a small butcher's shop you could buy black pudding in small pieces for a penny, and there were faggots, those Yorkshire rissoles of chopped liver. In the fish-and-chip shops you could get a piece of fish for twopence with a pennyworth of chips, except few people had the twopence to buy the fish. You could buy fish cakes: two slices of potato with a bit of fish in the middle, dipped in batter and fried – that cost a penny. The kids would get a pennyworth of chips and 'Can I have some of the bits?' and they would get half a portion of the batter bits that had been scraped off the side of the deep frier or had floated on top of the fat.

Boys wore clogs. They were lace-up ones, and men who were unemployed would put a design all over the leather; they did it with brass sprigs, which they hammered into the leather, then filed so smoothly on to the back of the boot that it wouldn't hurt a child's foot. The clogs would be brightly polished and the studs would shine. It was always my ambition to have a pair of clogs, but my mother would never let me have any; she felt it would be a sign of social disgrace if I didn't have shoes on my feet. But I played with a boy called Arthur who did have clogs, and when we went out to play he would put on my shoes and I would put on his clogs and we were both satisfied. Arthur's ambition was to have a pair of shoes.

Another special treat for me was to ride on the tram. It was only a halfpenny from where I lived to where Arthur lived, but because Arthur's mother couldn't afford the fares for him, not even the halfpenny, he had a little red disc which he used to hand to the conductor and get a ticket for it. I enjoyed riding on the tram with Arthur's disc almost as much as Arthur enjoyed having my halfpenny to pay his fare. The only thing I didn't want which Arthur had, and which many other boys had also, was the haircut. The clippers at the barber's would be run all over their heads until they were shaved nearly as close as Yul Brynner's, and there was a peculiar kind of tuft left at the front. Whether this was for decoration I never did find out, but it was as if there was a little brush growing out of their heads and looked anything but attractive.

If you walked through the streets at the back of the main road and into the entries between the back-to-back houses, you would see the men playing 'put and take'. This was a simple game played with a top, the top having six sides – one said 'put one' and another 'take one' then 'put two' . . . 'take two', 'put three' . . . 'take three'. They would play for matches or for halfpennies, and now and again for cigarettes; they would spin the top and it would tell the man who was spinning whether he could take from the kitty or whether he had to put in.

There were bookmakers everywhere, and bookies' runners; no bet was too small for them to take from a penny each way upwards. They always paid out. Bookmakers did well because with that kind of stake there was no point in backing the favourite.

I remember the poverty, yet I also remember the kindness and the generosity of all those people. Like the adversity during the war which made people stand together as a nation, the poverty around Oldham made those who suffered the poverty, hunger, degradation and deprivation of manliness and pride always prepared to give what little they had. I remember those people, kind and gentle to one another – the women old long before their time – and having one of the highest infant mortality rates in England.

Then there was Wakes Week, which came round once a year as the weekly holiday, though a majority of men in the town had been on an enforced holiday for two or three years. I remember Wakes Week, the fair on Tommyfield, the market of Oldham, the cobbled streets, the cobbled market-place, the roundabouts and the noise. I remember Mary Granelly who sold ice-cream. She was a huge lady, and for a penny you got a wafer commensurate with her size.

There were quacks of all kinds. It cost 2s. 6d. to go to the doctor's, so you didn't do that very often, especially if you were only getting 10s. a week dole for your wife, 12s. for yourself and 2s. for each child. So there was a man who could cure your cough; his medicine was also good, he said, if you had TB. He sold a lot because there were a lot of people with consumption. There was also a man who sold corn-cure. Everybody seemed to have corns, except those who wore clogs, and laid out on the stall for all to see were corns – big hard pieces of skin – that had been removed by his wondrous preparations. I particularly remember this man because he said that his was a secret preparation made out of snake oil, and that always impressed me because I had no idea where you got snake oil. Everyone used to stand around his stall listening to the man selling his wares and he appeared to know exactly what he was talking about, so I didn't like to show my ignorance by asking where snake oil came from.

My father would take me round the market. We would stand by one stall and watch a man who had big pans in which he boiled and made his own sweets. The smell of these pans came to your nostrils wherever you were in the market-place and it used to draw you towards it like a magnet. My father always bought me some of these sweets, which were sticky and tasted mainly of peppermint and aniseed. I am sure that today they would taste awful to my pampered palate, but then they tasted better than any other sweets I could remember.

On Saturday nights men auctioned everything left on their stalls, sweets, china, bedding, they were all there shouting while the naphtha flares hissed away lighting up their wares. There was always laughter around the stalls as men tried to get you to bid for a pair of sheets or a set of bone china which they said would cost you £20 in Lewis's in Manchester, though they were only asking 7s. 6d. People would stand near the meat stalls and the vegetable stalls late on Saturday night waiting for these wares to be sold at give-away prices, the bruised and battered greengrocery and the bones with a bit of meat left on. People would queue to hear the stallkeeper say, 'Here you are, missus, no it doesn't matter, love, I don't want your money', and you would hear them say, 'Thank you, master' . . . that word 'master' has for me always had a fearful ring to it ever since then. It was an echo from the days of the mill-owners and the overseers, a kind of acknowledge-ment of the servitude of those who had worked in the mills, worked in conditions which were not much better then, in the 1930s, than they had been in the early days of the Industrial Revolution . . . for those who had jobs in the mills. For the vast majority, a job of any kind, anywhere, was something to dream about. To have a job was not just to have a wage, even though the wage was at starvation rate; it was to be something apart, it was to be a man.

When I travelled on the tram with my father, we always went upstairs, and sometimes I would sit outside on the open front, on these open-ended tramcars you could shout to your friends from if you saw them in the street and they would all wave back. If it was cold, you would sit inside on wooden seats, and I would always sit near the window. As the tram clanged along you could look down on the women standing in the doorways with their arms folded, black shawls around their shoulders and black aprons tied in front. You could also see into the bedroom windows of the houses as you went by, and you could often see figures sitting there, white-faced men staring out through the windows. I wondered, as a boy, why they were there, and it was not until much later that I found out. Pneumonokoniosis, tuberculosis, or simply despair were the reasons why those men took to their beds.

All the world in Oldham looked much better when looked down upon from a tram. It looked more animated, more as if it were living; it was different from when you were walking among the people on the pavement, aware that the whole of the town and the people in it were dying and decaying. As a boy you wondered why, then gradually came to understand the anger of some men, the resignation of others.

When I went on the tram with my mother, however, we always went downstairs, and I would sit on the outside of the seat, not near the window. I liked going with my mother because she would take me into Lyons and buy me a big ice-cream, or we would have coffee and a meringue. I don't think my mother exactly approved of my father's taking me to the market and the aniseed sweets. I remember sitting alongside her and the tram clanging along; as you rode on the tram you would be shaken from side to side. If anyone was getting in the way of the tram, the driver had a bell which he rang by pressing a button with his foot.

One day I was on a tram with my mother, though I can't recall why or where we were going on this particular journey. The tram had stopped, and I looked at the people waiting to get on. There were six ladies, and I remember how white and pale they looked, their shawls over their heads. Such shawls were crocheted, and were always black. One of the ladies in the front carried a white box which appeared to me to be about two foot six inches long. It was about eighteen inches deep and not much wider. The driver of the tram looked back through his glass door from where he was standing and the conductor got down to help the lady up. She carried the white box past me and sat on the other side of the tram, another of the women sitting by her. The box was eased so that it rested on the knees of both women. Two

71

of the other women sat in the seat in front of her and two behind. The conductor rang his bell, but, I noticed, didn't go to collect their fares.

I nudged my mother. 'Be quiet and sit still,' she said.

'What is it, mother?' I asked. My mother just sat staring straight ahead. 'What are they doing?' Again I nudged her.

'Be quiet.'

I looked up at her. I think, looking back, that I had grown rather annoyed because she wouldn't answer me and that was unlike her; if you asked either her or my father a question, you always got an answer. Again I pressed her, 'Mother,' and this time she seemed to half-push me out of the seat as she stood up and in one movement transferred me from the outside seat into the one next to the window. She did it with considerable skill; there was no fuss, and nobody seemed to notice. The six ladies sat on and the tram clanged along for some time.

My mother, as if to make amends, had taken hold of my hand. Then the ladies turned their heads and looked at the conductor. He nodded and rang the bell. The tram began to slow, though the ladies didn't get up until it had stopped. The driver looked back through his window and took off his hat. The six ladies stood and the two in front took hold of the box, which appeared to be light enough. They carried it to the back of the tram and the conductor took off his hat while my mother made the sign of the cross. The six ladies got off the tram and walked up the road towards the cemetery, two in front with the box and four behind.

I had never seen a child's coffin before and today I can never see a funeral without remembering those six ladies and the tiny coffin.

That was the first impression I had of sorrow. The kind of sorrow that enters into you and chills you, the kind of sorrow you sense rather than feel, that is conveyed without words and without visible sign. The sorrow felt by those six ladies in their black shawls.

11 PENNY

Penny was sixteen years old, a tallish girl, slim and well proportioned. She had blonde hair which she wore in two plaits and they curved out from the side of her head. Her eyes, which were set wide apart, were flecked with green and she had a wide, humorous mouth.

Penny was said to be 'refractory in care', which really meant that she wouldn't stay anywhere she was put. She was said to be promiscuous, and it was also said that, apart from being in moral danger and likely to become pregnant, she was associating with people who were likely to get her into trouble with the law. It was also felt that someone might put her 'on the game'. Penny was highly intelligent with an I.Q. of 135 and she had a keen sense of humour. She was mature, she could discuss day-to-day happenings and she read the newspaper from cover to cover. She was friendly with the staff – 'It ain't your fault I am in here.' 'Whose fault is it then Penny?' 'I suppose it's my own bleeding fault, miss.'

One night I sat talking to her; she sat on the stairs and I on a little stool near a radiator.

'Are you cold?' I asked.

'No, I'm not cold.'

She had been showing me some paintings and drawings she had done in school that day. They were excellent. She had ability.

'Do you like them?' she asked.

'Very much.'

'Yes. They are not bad, don't think art is my subject though.'

'No? Why not?'

'No real creative talent,' she said. 'I can copy but I don't think
. . . well, I would make a fair draughtsman, I think.'

'What school did you go to, Penny?'

She told me. 'I went to another before that,' she said.

'Oh, did you?'

'Yes,' she said. I continued to look at the paintings. 'Do you
like art?'

'Yes, I do,' she replied.

'Do you ever go to the galleries?'

She nodded her head. 'Yes.'

'When do you go there?'

'I used to go on Saturday mornings mainly, I used to go to the
Tate.'

'Do you like the Tate?'

'Yes.'

'Why?'

'There is such a variety of painting. I don't think some of them
are art,' she said, 'but I like them.'

'Who did you go with?'

'I didn't go with anybody.'

'Why not?'

'Well, who would I go with from our building? They would
think I was bloody stupid . . . sorry for swearing.'

'That's all right.'

'But they would, you know, nobody from our buildings goes to
the Tate.'

'Do you tell anybody?'

'No. Me mum knows I go.'

'Have you ever taken her?'

'No. Me mum never goes out, well, only to the shops, you know,
but she never really goes out.'

'Not even with your father?'

'No, she never goes out with the old man.'

'Don't they get on together?'

'Yes, they get on fairly well together well, except when he gets
drunk.'

'Is that often?'

'No, not really.'

'When he does, does he get difficult?'

'No, he is not difficult, he makes a lot of noise and my mother tells him off.'

'What school did you say you went to?' I said, remembering what we had been talking about.

'I went to a grammar school'

'Did you?'

'Yes.'

'Did you like it?'

'Yes.'

'You left?'

'Yes.'

'Why?'

'Well, nobody else in our buildings went to a grammar school and, well, you feel a bit stupid really, in uniform . . . you know, everybody calls you names,everybody thinks you're daft for wanting to go to a grammar school.'

'So that's why you left?'

'Yes.'

'What do you want out of life, Penny?' I asked.

'What do I want?' she said. 'It's not a question of what I want, is it?'

'You will get what you want out of life.'

'It's all right for people like you, but not in our buildings, it's not.'

'For people like me, why people like me?'

'It's different, isn't it?'

'I don't know.'

'Well, it is. Probably where you lived was a bit posher.'

I tried to explain to her that although I hadn't lived in slums I didn't feel that I had lived anywhere quite as grand as Penny imagined.

'Well, you know what I mean.'

'No, I don't.'

'Well, it isn't what you want, is it? It's what you get and what happens.'

'What do you mean, what happens?'

'Well, it happens to all the girls in our buildings, and all the fellows really.'

'Is that why you ran away?'

75

'No, you see they said I was promiscuous,' and she pronounced the word correctly.

'Well, weren't you?'

'No, I wasn't. I had had it but only with . . . you see, Mr Hart, in our buildings it isn't like being up where the social workers come from or the teachers. You see, if a fellow takes you out where I come from, to the cinema or Battersea Park or anywhere really, when you come home you have to pay.'

'Pay? What do you mean you have to pay?'

'Well, you stand on the landing with your knickers in your hand.'

She said it in a matter-of-fact way.

'Do you mean you have to?'

'Yes.'

'But why?'

'Because it's our buildings, isn't it? That's the thing that's done, and if you didn't, nobody would take you out and you would be chicken.'

'Couldn't you go outside your buildings to find your friends?'

'No.'

'Why not?'

'You couldn't come back to our buildings. I couldn't very well take them back there, could I?'

'Why not?'

'Well, they wouldn't have it.'

'Who, your parents?'

'No, the fellows and the other girls, in any case, they would . . . you don't do that, you stick to your own.'

'Are you telling me that if you went out with seven different fellows on seven different nights of the week, and each time from your own buildings, that when you came back that would be expected of you?'

'Yes,' she said. 'That is why you get yourself a fellow.' Penny was a very moral young woman who took one fellow rather than be passed around God knows how many other young men, but this was not immoral, this was the norm for their buildings.

'Don't you believe,' I said to her, 'that we have some say in our destiny and the way we wish to lead our lives?'

'No, not really.'

'What would you like to do?'

76

'I don't know.'

'What do you hope for?'

'Well, I suppose if I don't get sent away I'll go back home to me mum. I really love me mum,' she said, 'and I miss her.'

'Do you talk much to your mother?'

'Oh yes. I can tell my mother about anything. My mother tells me too about things, you know.'

'About what kind of things?'

'Well, about her life really.'

'What does she tell you?'

'Oh, what it was like in the buildings, you know, years ago.'

'What was it like?'

'Don't think it was much different except that the flats were a bit newer.'

'What will you do when you go home?'

'Get a job, I suppose.'

'Doing what?'

'I don't know, maybe in a shop or whatever is going.'

'Will you like that?'

'No, no not really but you have to make do, haven't you?'

'What about later on?'

'Well, I suppose I shall get married really.'

'Will you like that?'

'Yes. I think that would be fine, well, it would be all right for a couple of years anyway.'

'What do you mean, for a couple of years?'

'Well, we will enjoy ourselves, won't we?'

'You mean, you and your husband?'

'Yes. It will be all right until I fall for a kid.'

'What then, wouldn't you like to have a child?'

'Yes, I would like one, but . . .'

'Why would it be bad for you if you had a child?'

'Well, I suppose when you are pregnant they start going out with other women, anyway . . . he wouldn't be able to go out. I suppose me mother would look after the baby.'

'Would she?'

'Yes, but it's not the same then, is it?'

I looked at Penny as she sat there. She seemed to me to be as much a prisoner in her buildings as anywhere else she might spend her life – she was more closed in there than she was in the remand

77

home. Her whole life was encompassed by it, and she knew it and understood it. It appeared that she had two years to look forward to – two years of married life when she thought she would be happy. The rest would be spent bringing up her own children who would have no more to look forward to than she had had.

'If you go to an approved school, you will at least get yourself an education.'

'Yes, I suppose so.'

'But I still don't understand why you ran away.'

'Well, they were implying that I was a slag and that I was sleeping around, but I wasn't and I resented that very much,' she said. 'They were going to come and take me and I didn't think it was fair.'

'So what then?'

'Well, I went on the run and I went up West, but you know, Mr Hart, that lot up there aren't going to give you anything for nothing, are they? I was glad in the end when they caught up with me.'

'Why didn't you . . . ?'

'I couldn't give myself up.'

'Why not?'

'I suppose my pride and . . . well, my mates in the . . .'

'In the buildings,' I said and she laughed.

'Yes, in the buildings, they would have thought I was bloody daft.'

In time Penny went to court and was committed to an approved school. She came back and we sat again and talked.

'I won't stay,' she said.

'You will only get yourself into further trouble, remember what you told me before – the only people who are going to take care of you are the ones who will be wanting something in return.'

'Yes, I suppose so.'

'Why don't you get yourself some "O"-levels and then think about what you are going to do?'

'From there? Well, I'll think about it.'

Penny would spend long periods of time just sitting in a chair with her feet curled up underneath her, staring out of the window.

'You are a right stuck-up cow,' said one girl to her. 'Don't you think we are good enough, is that why you never to speak to us?'

Penny just looked at her.

'Have I got to go away?' she said to me one day.

'You could appeal.'

'Yes, I could.'

'Well, if you are so "agin" it, why don't you appeal? It was the first time you had ever been before a court.'

'Do you think I would win it?'

'I don't know whether you would win it, but I would think you stood an even chance.'

'How soon do I have to make up my mind?'

'In two weeks,' I replied. 'I'll tell you what, think about it and tell me at the end of the week.'

I saw Penny again, I remember, on a Sunday evening. It was winter time and dark and she was sitting in a chair with her feet pulled up underneath her.

'What would you do?' she asked.

'I don't know.'

'What do you mean, you don't know? You are supposed to know everything, to give us all the advice.'

'Well, I don't know what I would do if I were you. The situation would be different and I would be angry like you are,' I said.' I don't know, I can only tell you what I think you should do.'

'What's that?'

'Get yourself an education, think about what you want to do in the future, then get yourself a better job than working in a shop. There must be more to life than the two years you told me about. You might be happy.'

'What about me mum? I wanted to go home to my mother. I really do miss her.'

'I don't know, but I would have thought that if you got yourself a reasonable job you might be able to do more for her, you might be better able to care for her.'

'Do you think so?'

'I would have thought so.'

Penny had discussions with psychiatrists, psychologists and house staff; she didn't appeal and she went to the approved school. She settled well and worked hard. I received letters from her, and when she was on leave she would phone me. She subsequently left the school having got five 'O'-levels, and the headmistress told me that Penny had asked if she could stay on for a period and try to get some 'A'-levels. She did, and a place was found for her in a

79

college. Penny worked hard. She is what people may call a success of the system. She now has a professional job and a small flat of her own, and she has never gone back to the buildings. She came to see me one day.

'Are you happy, Penny?' I asked her.

'Yes, I think so, though I feel out of place.'

'Why out of place?'

'I feel out of place, I'm always out of place. I look at the bright young men I work with and occasionally go to bed with – I've got a profession, I've got a nice flat and I've got a nice salary – you gave me all these things, but you took away all the things I knew, including my mother.'

'Did we do that to you? Is that what we did?'

'Yes. Oh, I'm better off in lots of ways – I'm not pregnant or have four kids and a husband out screwing somebody else. I'm not waiting at home jealous and wanting money, and wondering if he will bring it in. I've got the things you talked about – you know, the security, the middle-class cake.'

'Aren't you happy?'

'No.'

'Were you ever happy?'

'Yes, I was happy when I was at home in the buildings with me mum. Remember asking me about going to the Tate? I used to go and then go home and tell her all about it. Yes, I was happy with me mum, and anyway, if I'd stayed in the buildings I wouldn't have known any better; you see, the thing I hate most about what has happened to me is that I am ashamed of coming from the buildings.'

I often think about Penny and wonder what else could have been done. Is what she's got any better than what she had? She had a mother she loved, still loves, but there was once a time when there was nothing about her mother which made her feel ashamed. Now the buildings and her mother are one and the same. 'You see,' she said, 'when you start being ashamed of where you live, you start being ashamed of the people who live there.'

At least if she had gone back she would have had her mother and her children to love. We gave her a career and we took away everything else.

12 NESTA

Nesta was a tall, well-proportioned girl. She was pretty and had long, dark, wavy hair. I remember she had well-shaped hands, the kind of hands which appear to have a mind and life of their own and emphasize all that the person has to say, with gestures which are positive but which appear to belong to the hands and not to the rest of the person. She had been in care for many years, during which she had had about nine moves. She was fifteen, alleged to be cheeky, very promiscuous and 'incapable of making relationships', according to the social history which I received before Nesta came to us.

Like so many deprived children, Nesta just walked in and behaved as if she had been there all her life. She walked around taking stock of this large, early-Victorian monstrosity which was now the home of fifty children. She learned her way about and her conversation was, 'Yes, miss', 'No, miss', as she sat there taking in the atmosphere and the people and their attitudes. I suppose today one would think of a computer soaking up information like a sponge. Nesta weighed up each individual member of staff along with the other children, and it was obvious that there wasn't much we could have told her about any of the other children. She could probably have told us more about the way they thought than we were ever likely to learn.

Nesta got on well with the housemother responsible for the girls. She (Nesta) had a great sense of humour and was able to

81

poke fun at people around her; her remarks were sometimes funny, but could be too near to the truth for comfort. She didn't attempt to do any of the things she was alleged to have done previously, such as going out and not coming back. She seemed to be content – like so many deprived adolescents – to make a fuss of the young children, to help bath them and put them to bed. And so, for some weeks, Nesta settled extremely well.

I remember that the first occasion when Nesta's problems were thrust upon us was on a Saturday evening. Suddenly I could hear quite a lot of noise coming from the road outside, and one of the staff said that there were a lot of boys gathered outside the railings. As I went outside the crowd seemed to be getting bigger by the second, so I walked round to see what it was they were looking at. Up on a balcony in the front of the building was Nesta wearing nothing but her pants, and laughing and waving to the crowd of boys. When she saw me she ran like mad back into her bedroom. The boys continued to shout and cheer for Nesta, and created a great disturbance. I asked them to move, but they took not the slightest notice; they were waiting for Nesta to give an encore. Then some of the neighbours came out and in much more forceful and colourful language told the boys to be on their way . . . and they went.

I went inside to find Nesta, who was, by this time, in the bath. When she had finished she came down to see me.

'What was all that about?' I asked.

'I was just nipping along – you know we have a wardrobe on the other side of the balcony there.'

'Yes,' I said.

'I was just going over there when I saw one of the boys and he saw me and shouted so I waved back.'

'Yes, but you know . . . while you were undressed . . .'

'Didn't really think, sir,' she said.

'Well you must have thought when you saw a crowd gather.'

'It was all a bit of a giggle.'

I told her that young ladies of fifteen and a half should be a little more modest and that it wasn't the thing to do . . . She listened to me quite politely. 'Sorry, Mr Hart,' she said. 'It won't happen again.'

A week or two went by without further incident and I began to think that it was perhaps just a giggle, as Nesta had said. Indeed,

I had forgotten all about the incident until one Friday evening when the crowd gathered again. This time I didn't bother to go out, I went upstairs with some of the staff to find that Nesta had gone one stage further; she didn't even have her pants on this time.

When she saw the staff she grabbed her dressing-gown and came back through. This time her attitude was a little different: truculent and rather aggressive. 'What the bleeding hell' had it got to do with us anyway. She 'bloody well wanted to go around naked' – it was her body and no one was going to stop her. Then, suddenly, Nesta burst into tears. She was an attractive youngster and one realized that the one thing she was aware of was her appearance – her figure. She was neat and tidy in her dress and was always bathing and doing her hair. It seemed pointless to make a meal out of what had happened in view of her distress, and the younger staff talked to her. Nesta said she only did it for fun.

Again some weeks went by, and the summer months were upon us. The children would go to the park across the road to play, and Nesta went with them. One morning a policewoman came and said, 'Look, we have had a complaint.'

'Oh yes,' I said. 'What about?'

'One of your girls.'

'Girls? Why, what have they been doing?'

'Well, some of the neighbours say that one of your girls is soliciting over in the park.'

'Don't be silly, they are only twelve- and thirteen-year-olds.'

'Haven't you got a girl older than that?'

Nesta.

'We don't want to do anything about it, but perhaps you could see to it, would you?'

I agreed and took a walk over into the park that afternoon, but Nesta was nowhere to be seen. I walked out of another gate and along the side of the park where there was a narrow path that went up to the back of some houses and through to the main road. Standing on the corner of this passageway was a group of women, and walking up and down, not far away, was Nesta. She had acquired a long blue coat and was wearing a pair of high-heeled shoes. I walked over to her. She gave a sideways flick of her head and walked up the narrow passageway, and for some reason which

I have never been able to fathom, I followed her. There was an opening into some trees, and as I walked up there was Nesta, complete with blanket, which she rolled up and put under the hedge. She took off her coat, rolled it up and put it under the hedge; then she picked something up from the ground, put on her shoes and walked through the hedge again. Again, I followed her. The whole procedure only took two or three minutes, and Nesta walked ahead of me back to the children's home.

As I went past the group of ladies standing on the corner, they began to call me rude names and tell me I should be ashamed of myself and what a horrible and revolting man I was. I suddenly realized what I had done. . . . These ladies had obviously misunderstood my motives in following Nesta. I think that was one of the most embarrassing walks I have ever taken and it was a day or so before I could see the funny side of it, though everyone else with whom I worked thought that it was a great joke.

When I came to talk to Nesta, she didn't deny her activities and made no excuses for them. I had no idea what to say to this terribly unhappy youngster who sat before me. People on the staff talked to her and she came to see me again.

'I'm sorry,' she said. 'It weren't fair what I was doing, because it only gets you a bad name and the other kids in this place and I really wouldn't want to do that,' and, as I looked at her, I knew that she meant it. But there didn't appear to be any level at which we could help her or touch her. Her behaviour became increasingly bizarre and there were more occasions when Nesta undressed herself and gathered the crowd of boys. She was seen by the psychiatrist, who could not find that she was depressed, just a very deprived, damaged youngster.

Then neighbours reported her behaviour to a local councillor and a meeting was called to discuss Nesta. She knew that this was going on and her behaviour became even more outrageous. It was finally decided that she should be taken before the court as being 'refractory in care' and with a recommendation that she should be placed in what was then termed an approved school.

I had to go to court with Nesta. I was called into the box and took the oath. The magistrate asked me, 'Why do you want to send her to an approved school?' I said that I didn't wish to send her to an approved school, but the problem was that we didn't know where to put Nesta to be of any assistance to her. While giving my evidence I was asked to describe her behaviour, which I did in a rather reluctant and hesitant way; it was the first time I had ever given evidence in any kind of court. The magistrate looked at me rather angrily . . . this very deprived girl being brought before the court . . . and then he turned to Nesta.

'Have you anything to say to what Mr Hart has said, Nesta?'

'Yes, I have,' she said.

'What is it?'

'He is a bloody liar.'

He turned to me. 'Have you anything to say to that?'

It appeared to me that there was very little that one could say, and I tried to point out that all I had said could be substantiated. But it was quite obvious that the magistrate was not, if he could help it, going to send Nesta to an approved school. Looking back over the years I hold his judgement good – her years in care had left her totally deprived, and further institutional care with an emphasis on training was contra-indicated. At the time, however, I felt that the magistrate's antagonism was directed towards me personally. Again looking back, perhaps I was for him the symbol of this child's mismanagement and the cause of her unhappiness.

'You had better go away,' he said, 'and come back in a week, and when you come back you had better have some representation here.'

'Representation?' I said.

'Yes, you had better get a solicitor to represent the local authority. Case adjourned for one week.'

So we went back.

'Sorry I got you into trouble,' said Nesta.

'I wasn't really in trouble Nesta,' I said, 'but what made you say I was lying?'

'I had to, didn't I? I couldn't bloody well say it was the truth, I would cut my own throat, wouldn't I?'

We returned to court the following week armed with a solicitor, who, prior to going to court, had taken me through the evidence. I went into the box and I went through my evidence again.

Nesta was standing there listening to it all. I could imagine what her feelings were as I looked at this very pale and controlled girl and realized how angry she was. I realized, too, that the magistrate was very much on her side and that, if he could, he was going to prevent this girl being sent to any approved school. He asked many searching questions of me and I felt that he was trying to trip me by his very skilful questioning. He managed to elicit from me that this was a very deprived girl who didn't need approved school care, a girl who required affection, understanding, concern and support. This took a long time, and then he turned to Nesta.

'Now, Nesta. What do you think?'

At this Nesta exploded. She rushed towards the bench where the magistrate was sitting and shouted, 'I don't think, and if you think you can send me to an approved school or anywhere else you ugly old, fucking old bastard, you can get it out of your head because I shan't stay.'

She then poured out a string of obscenities directed towards everyone sitting on the bench, took a deep breath, put a hand in her macintosh pocket and took out a packet of chewing-gum, put a piece in her mouth and chewed it, then gave the magistrates the 'V' sign. I have never seen three people look quite so shocked. A hush went over the courtroom and everyone sat back to wait and see what would happen. Nesta went to an approved school.

I left the court and went to see Nesta in the waiting-room on her way to the remand home.

'Hello, Mr Hart,' she said.

'Hello, Nesta.'

'That told them, didn't it?'

'Yes,' I said. 'It most certainly did.'

'Yes, I feel better for that, you know.'

'Yes, I should imagine you do.'

'I'm sorry I called you a liar.'

We sat there and Nesta smoked her cigarette.

'Will you write to me?' she asked.

'Yes, I will write.'

'Will you tell Auntie' (the housemother who had cared for her) 'that I will write?'

'Yes,' I said. She stood up and I stood up and she leaned against me and cried. Her whole body shook. Yet when she drew away she was dry-eyed, there were no tears left, they had been used up a long time ago.

13   PRUDENCE

Prudence lived in a Roman Catholic children's home. The good nuns who looked after her were very fond of her, but Prudence, to say the least, wasn't the easiest child in the world. First, she was educationally subnormal, and secondly, she believed that taking other people's property was not stealing but simply providing herself with the comforts that others possessed, but for which she herself didn't have the money. Prudence had been before the Juvenile Court on many occasions. Each time the sister who cared for her went along and spoke up on her behalf, and each time the magistrates agreed that it would be wrong for Prudence to be moved or sent to an approved school. The sisters were obviously very fond of her, but so far hadn't been able to convince her of that commandment, 'Thou shalt not steal'.

Prudence was also reaching the age at which she was beginning to have serious doubts about Roman Catholicism, particularly with regard to its dogma and to the fact that it was obligatory to go to Mass on Sundays and to communion once a month. The good sisters in the children's home made no more of the Catholic faith than parents in an ordinary Catholic household, but, even so, Prudence was very reluctant to do many of the things which the nuns felt a good Catholic girl should do. A social worker friend of mine who worked for a local authority, but who also worked on a voluntary basis for this Catholic organization, was approached for advice about Prudence.

'It's not that she won't go to communion, and it's not that she won't go to confession, it's just that she's so emphatic and so difficult about it and, well, the other children are beginning to follow her lead. We wondered,' they said to the social worker, 'whether you could have a talk with her.'

The social worker, who was also Catholic, felt that perhaps this was a case in which she could be of some help.

'Now Prudence,' she said, 'why don't you want to go to communion?'

She explained to Prudence about the Mass and what the meaning of communion was. Prudence sat and listened, eyes cast down, and said that she knew all that and she knew that the others went, but she knew that God would bless her and she didn't intend to go.

'I ain't going, miss.'

'Well, will you tell me why not?' asked the social worker.

'Ain't going to confession at the church down there.'

'Why not?'

'I ain't going because when I go in that box the priest knows who I am and I get embarrassed.'

'Why do you get embarrassed? He probably doesn't know who you are anyway.'

'Well, I think he knows who I am and I ain't going.'

The social worker talked some more to young Prudence, but she was adamant, she wasn't going.

A little while later Prudence again appeared before the court for stealing from Woolworth's. The social worker went along to the court with the nuns and once again the magistrate felt that she should be returned to the children's home. Prudence was always a little worried about going to court and afterwards was always a little quiet, so the social worker thought it would be a good time to have another word with her about going to confession and communion. Again Prudence listened politely.

'Ain't going to that church,' she said.

'Will you go to another one?'

Prudence thought for a little while. 'Where?'

'Well we could go to the town and have some lunch and then we could go to a big church where nobody would know you, and maybe afterwards we could have an outing, do something you might like to do.'

Again Prudence gave this some thought. 'All right,' she said, and the following Saturday the social worker arrived to take her up to London. They went and had a meal and Prudence appeared to be quite happy and relaxed. She walked along holding the social worker's hand until eventually they arrived at Westminster Cathedral.

'See, it's a big church, Prudence, and there are lots of people going to confession.'

Prudence looked at the confessional and at all the people kneeling outside awaiting their turn, and then she nodded.

'So now you will go to confession here, Prudence?'

'Yes, miss.'

The social worker dipped her fingers into the holy water and made the sign of the cross and then the two of them walked down to the confessional. They knelt in one of the pews and Prudence shut her eyes, apparently saying her prayers. Then she sat up on the seat.

'Do you know what you do when you go into the confessional, Prudence?'

'Yes, miss.'

'And do you know how to begin your confession?'

'Yes, miss.'

'Do you know an act of contrition?'

Prudence turned to look at the social worker. 'An act of contrition, miss?'

'Yes.'

'No, miss.'

'Of course, you must do, Prudence. It begins, "Oh my God . . ." '

'Oh yes, I know all about that,' said Prudence.

They sat a little longer, and then it was Prudence's turn to enter the confessional. She got up and walked past all those who were either kneeling or sitting waiting to make their confession, looking straight ahead. Everyone tried to give the impression that they couldn't hear the whispering going on in the box, until the time came for Prudence to say her act of contrition. Her voice came loud and clear from within the box. 'I swear by Almighty God, the evidence I shall give shall be the truth, the whole truth and nothing but the truth.'

The social worker sat, appalled. All the others waiting turned to look at each other, which added to her discomfort, until suddenly they all burst into laughter which they tried to control as Prudence came out of the confessional.

'I've been, miss. I've gotta say three "Hail Marys", and two "Our Fathers".'

'Yes, Prudence,' said the social worker.

Prudence knelt down and said her three 'Hail Marys' and her two 'Our Fathers' for her penance. Then they both stood up, went out of the pew, genuflected and walked past all the others waiting to make their confession. All of them turned to smile at Prudence.

'I like this place,' she said.

'Why Prudence?'

'All the people who come here are so friendly.'

14 MABEL

Mabel arrived in a car escorted by four police-men. She was brought in through the door, handcuffed and fighting. I stood there and looked at this child in her white macintosh and high boots, and it was hard to realize that she had been responsible for the death of another person. A policeman took off the hand-cuffs. She looked at me and then at the police.

'I'm hungry,' she said.

Two members of staff came forward and said hello and I asked them to take her along for something to eat. The policeman went out and helped in another police officer, a man in his fifties. He looked shaken and white. The girl had kicked him very badly on the journey, but I think he was more upset by her behaviour in general than by the kick he had received. We put a dressing on his leg and found them all some tea.

'We take her again on Monday,' one of them said.

I nodded and went off to find Mabel. She was sitting at the table having her tea.

'Do you like television?' she asked.

'Yes, I do at times.'

'What programmes do you like?'

'I don't know really. What programmes do you like?'

'I like programmes about the Saint.'

'Do you now? Why is that?'

'There is a lot of fighting in them.'

'Do you like fighting?'

'Yes.'

She had finished her meal and she stood up. She was an attractive girl, dark, and not very tall, five feet one or so. She stood very close to me and looked up at me. 'What would you do if I kicked you?'

'Well, you're not going to kick me, are you?'

She stared at me for a few seconds. 'No.'

She picked up a knife from the table and turned to one of the staff. 'If I hit you with this, what would you do?'

'I don't know,' said the member of staff. 'I don't think I'd like it very much.'

Mabel put the knife back on the table and walked over to the window to look out. 'Where will I sleep?'

'I'll show you your room if you like.'

'Will I have a room to myself?'

'Yes.'

'Not like those bloody cells that . . . ?'

'No.'

She walked up the stairs with us and was shown her room. Again she went to the window. 'It'll soon be dark, won't it?'

'Yes.'

'I don't like the dark.'

'Why not?'

'Well, you can't see what's moving when it's dark.'

'How do you mean, you can't see what's moving?'

'Things that are moving and people. People in the dark can stand and look at you and you don't know.'

The doctor arrived to see her.

'Who are you?'

'I'm a doctor.'

'What do you want?'

'I just want to see that you are all right.'

'Why? Because I kicked a bloody policeman? I always kick policemen.'

'Why?'

'I don't like them.'

'Have they ever done anything to you to make you not like them?'

'No, but they'll take me to the police court, won't they?'

'Yes.'

'They'll tell everybody what I've done.'

'Well, they won't say anything they don't believe to be true.'

'But they will tell everybody about me and everybody will know what I've done. They'll make it bad for my parents.'

'They won't make it bad for your parents.'

'Oh yes, they will. When people know about me, they'll know about my mother and father, and people will talk about them. All because I . . .'

'Because you what?'

'You know.'

The doctor looked at her as she stood there. She had a piece of balsa wood in her hands which one of the other girls had been carving and she snapped it in half as she stood.

'Do you sleep well?'

'No.'

'Why not?'

'I don't sleep because I dream and I don't want to dream.'

'So you try to stay awake?'

'No, I don't. I just don't sleep well.'

'Maybe I could give you something to help you to sleep, and you wouldn't dream. If I did, would you take it?'

'I don't know.'

'Oh well, I'll write you up for something. We'll see what we can do. Good night, Mabel, I'll see you tomorrow.'

The doctor walked to the door. Mabel drew back her foot and I looked at her. 'What would you do if I kicked you?' she said to the doctor.

'Well, if you kicked me hard, I'd probably yell,' and he smiled. Mabel laughed back at him.

That night after she had bathed and was in her bedroom one of the staff went to give her the medicine.

'I ain't taking it,' she said. 'I'll take it off that bloke.'

'Which bloke?'

'The one with the pipe.'

The member of staff phoned me and said Mabel would take the medicine only from me. I went up to her bedroom and she sat up in the bed.

'Here you are,' I said. 'Take this.'

'Does it taste nasty?'

'I don't know really. Some of the other girls who have had it say it tastes a bit bitter.'

'Give me a sweet, then,' she said.

One of the staff went away and came back with some fruit sweets. I gave her the medicine, which she drank, then I offered her one of the sweets.

'Which colour shall I have?' she asked.

'I don't know, which colour would you like?'

'I'll have a red one.'

She took the red one, undid the paper and put the sweet into her mouth. Then she smoothed all the creases out of the cellophane paper, folded it neatly and kept on folding it until she could fold it no more. She sat with it in the middle of her hand, palm upwards, and then held out her hand for me to take the paper.

'Give it back to me tomorrow morning,' she said.

'What, the paper?'

'Yes.'

'What do you want it back for?'

'I want it.'

'It's time you went to sleep now,' I said, and she lay down in the bed and pushed the pillows up.

'Do you know any prayers?' she asked.

'Yes. Don't you?'

'Yes.'

'Which one do you know?' I asked.

'I know a lot.'

'Well, say them, then. I'll go if you don't want me to be here.'

'No. You say one for me.'

I looked at the girl. 'No, why me? You say one.'

'No, I can't. I can't say prayers, I never say prayers.'

'What prayer would you like?'

' "Our Father",' she said.

I sat at the end and said the 'Our Father'. Suddenly she closed her eyes and began to cry, then just as suddenly she opened them and said, 'I'm bloody daft, I shouldn't cry, I'm bloody daft, why should I cry?'

'Do you want the light out or do you want me to leave it on?' I asked.

'Will you leave it on?'

'Yes, if you want me to. Good night.'

94

'What's your name?' she asked, and I told her.

'Good night,' she said.

When I went back to see her the following day, Mabel was walking around the sitting-room with a chair in her hands.

'What would you do if I hit you over the head with this?' she was saying to one of the staff.

'I probably wouldn't be in a position to do much if you did that, but then, you wouldn't want to do it, would you?' she asked.

'No.'

During the whole of that day Mabel restlessly walked round the sitting-room, picking up objects and putting them down; sometimes she would go to the wastepaper basket and take out the sweet boxes, rip them up until they were like confetti, then put them back in the bin again.

There was a war film on television that night, and as the machine-guns fired and men dashed forward and were shot, Mabel bounced up and down in her chair, screaming with delight. The other girls sat quietly, watching her with obvious apprehension.

Two or three days later a member of staff came to me. 'I hate to say this, but Mabel frightens me.'

'Do you mean her violence?'

'No. It's not her violence, I just can't explain it.'

'Do you want to come out of that group?'

'I don't know. Maybe . . . I don't know. If I want to, will you take me out?'

'Yes,' I said.

Mabel's parents visited her. They were two extremely quiet and gentle people, utterly bewildered by the events which had taken place and looking as if they were in a state of shock. Mabel behaved with them as if she were five years old, laughing and sitting first on one's knee and then on the other's, and undoing the presents they had brought for her. When the time came for them to go, they said, 'We'll see you tomorrow, Mabel.'

'Where?' she asked suddenly, and her whole attitude changed.

'We'll be at the court when you come tomorrow.'

'Yes.'

I walked down the stairs with the parents.

'I don't understand it,' said the father. 'I just don't understand what's happening – I don't even believe it's happening.'

There was not much that one could say to them. It was difficult to try and convey sympathy for they were not really aware of me or any other people. We shook hands and they left to go home.

'Do you like my mother and father?' Mabel asked me later that day.

'Yes, they seem to be very nice people.'

'Yes, there's nothing my dad can't do.'

'Isn't there?'

'No. You ought to see all the things he's done in the house – smashing things. He decorated my bedroom and put shelves up.'

'I'm sure it was very nice.'

'Yes, they'll have to leave there now.'

'Why?'

'Because of me, because of me.'

Suddenly she began to cry and no amount of comforting could stop the tears. I don't believe I have ever seen anyone cry as Mabel did: it was as if all the pain and all the guilt of all the ages poured out of this fifteen-year-old girl. Just as suddenly she stopped and went to the window.

'What time is it?'

'About half past eight.'

'It's cold out, isn't it?'

'Yes.'

'When you're dead you are cold, aren't you?'

'Yes.'

'But you can't feel the cold?'

'No, you can't feel the cold.'

'And you can't see or hear?'

'No, none of those things.'

'Will the cold go away?'

'How do you mean?'

'When you are dead, do you stop feeling cold, do you stop being cold?'

'No.'

'When I go to court . . .'

'Yes?'

'They . . . I'll have to sit in that box.'

'Yes.'

'I'll pretend it's a flower-box.'

'You mean the box you'll be sitting in?'

'Yes. I'll pretend it's all full of flowers, that they're all around me and I'm sitting in the middle where no one can see me, and I won't have to hear what's going on or listen, will I?'

'Not if you don't want to.'

'When they bury him . . . ?' she asked suddenly.

'Yes?'

'They wouldn't let me send flowers, would they?'

'I don't know.'

'My mum and dad will.'

'Yes, I'm sure they will.'

'And they'll hate me, won't they?'

'Who.'

'All the others, all those people, his mother and his father.'

'They will be very sad. Sometimes people are so sad that, well . . . they don't hate.'

'Do you think I ought to say I'm sorry?'

'Are you sorry?'

'Yes, I'm sorry. I want to say I'm sorry.'

'If you want to say it, you can say it.'

'If I do, they'll think I'm just saying it because . . .'

'No, I'm sure they won't.'

'He'd no need to die, no need to die,' she said and jumped up and began to pace up and down the room. She was like an animal looking for somewhere to run and hide. 'Do you hate me?' she said suddenly.

'No, I don't hate you.'

'Do you like me?'

'Yes, I like you.'

'You'd say that whether you did or not.'

'No, I wouldn't say it if I didn't mean it.'

'Do you think people would want to know me now?'

'Yes.'

'Do you think my parents . . . ?'

'Your parents care for you very much.'

'I'm going to bed now,' she said.

I left her room and one of the staff went in to her, and when she was in bed I took in her medicine.

'What colour sweet do you want?'

'A green one.'

I gave her the green sweet, and again she smoothed out the cellophane paper and began to fold it.

'Do you know,' she said, 'I didn't dream last night.'

'I'm glad.'

'I won't dream tonight, will I?'

'No.'

'Would you stay in the room until I go to sleep, miss?' she said to the staff member.

'Yes.'

She sat on the top of her bed then, and said, 'I left something downstairs.'

'What is it? I'll get it for you,' said the member of staff.

'No, I'll get it.'

They went down the stairs and came back with a teddy bear.

'Does it belong to anyone?' asked Mabel, who was carrying it.

'It belongs to you now if you want it,' said the member of staff.

'Yes,' she said, 'I'd like it.'

She put it in the bed and then got in herself. 'I had a teddy at home.'

'Did you have it a long time?'

'Ever since I was . . . well I can't remember how long I had it.'

'Why don't you ask your mother and father to bring it in for you, and then you could have it with you?'

She looked at the teddy in the bed. 'No, I'll keep this one. He doesn't know anything about me so we can be friends. If I don't tell him, he won't know, and I'll be able to talk to him about other things . . . new things. Maybe one day I will be able to tell him about them but, well, he might like me by then.'

She lay down in the bed, and the member of staff tucked her in. I went out of the room, and she called me back. I stood at the end of her bed.

'I'll go away for a long time, won't I?'

'I don't know what will happen in court, but you will for a time, anyway.'

'I think I'd like that, I think I'd like to go away. It would be nice to go away and go where it was always dark, always dark. No one could see you . . .'

15 TERRY

I was sent for by my boss and asked to go to an establishment which was having considerable difficulties. The previous head, who had been there for many years, had retired, leaving a gap which left the girls with a feeling of insecurity and uncertainty.

'I'd like you and your wife to go there just for two or three months to run it,' he said. 'There has just been a little difficulty down there.'

The day I arrived I walked up the drive to this new building and saw a number of policemen sitting on the steps.

'Hello,' I said. 'What's going on?'

'Oh, nothing much, just had a bit of trouble, but we're all right now.' They all looked very red in the face, but smoked their cigarettes and straightened their uniforms before getting into their van.

I rang the bell and went in through the glass doors. Nobody appeared to take much notice of me for a time, and eventually a lady whom I knew spotted me and said she was pleased to see me. She told me they had been having a bit of trouble, but, now that I was there, all would be well. I walked around and saw windows boarded up and doors that didn't appear to be on their hinges. The members of staff looked at me without a great deal of welcome or enthusiasm, I thought.

'Are you the new caretaker?' said one. I began to get a distinctly chilled feeling.

That evening I took a walk along to the main house. I could hear screaming and shouting and a girl came dashing by. She ran towards the closed door that led to the surgery, and as she couldn't get through the door she drew back her foot and kicked the door panel out.

I stood with what must have been a look of complete amazement at this exhibition. She was a big girl and she turned to me and said, 'What are you doing here, mate?'

'Well, I've come to work here,' I said.

'What are you going to do?'

'I'm going to run the place.'

'Oh, you poor bleeder,' she said. 'Where are you going now?'

'I'm looking for my office,' I said.

'I'll take you, mate,' she said.

She pushed the panel of the door she had just kicked through until she made enough space for herself, then she bent down, went through and peeped from the other side. 'It's through here, the door on your right.'

Whereupon, she dashed up the stairs.

To say the least, I felt a little unnerved. As the days went by a number of the girls moved on, but by this time the place had a reputation – the reputation being that if you were sent there, you had a hell of a good time wrecking the place.

Terry came. She was intelligent, a kind of pretty, elf-like girl who had been indulging in black magic with some people in Sussex. She talked about Pan and of having seen him with a blue light shining round him, and she drew crosses upside down. She had been missing from home for a long time, and her parents, who seemed to be nice people, had become very worried about her and had informed the police. They had been looking for her for months.

Terry was a leader, petite and bright, but bigger and tougher girls did as she said. They were also a little afraid of her because she made her own ouija board with a wine glass and an alphabet and was prepared to talk to the devil for them, if they wanted her to. Interestingly enough, nobody did. She was a girl who had a sense of humour and also a sense of fair play. Although she made life difficult, she also knew when she had won and never went any further to prove the point.

It was late one night when the night staff phoned me to say that the girls were being very difficult. I went along and saw girls going in and out of their rooms at such a fast rate it looked like a Micky Mouse cartoon. It took about two hours to calm them and quieten them enough to enable us to talk them into some sort of reasonable behaviour. The girls were by this time quite exhausted, and I stood leaning on a window-sill in a long passage, smoking a cigarette and talking to one of the staff.

'I never saw Terry,' she said suddenly.

'Oh my God, she's sure to have gone.'

I went along to her room with a member of staff and knocked on the door, not expecting an answer. An angelic voice from inside called, 'Come in,' and propped up on her elbow, her head resting on her hand, was Terry.

'You don't trust little Terry,' she said. 'You thought I'd run away.'

'No, little Terry. Never. I've just come along to say how pleased I am that you didn't make any trouble tonight.'

She looked half-smilingly at me as I stood in the doorway. The cigarette tasted foul, so I thought I would try my pipe. I threw the cigarette out of the window, filled my pipe and looked at Terry.

My only excuse for the remarks I made was that I was tired. I looked at her. 'You know, Terry,' I said, 'I've been married for sixteen years, and after three weeks here I've come to the conclusion that I know nothing about women.'

Terry looked at me for a minute. 'How long did you say you had been married?' she asked.

'Sixteen years,' I said.

'By Christ,' she said, 'Mrs Hart must have liked old men.'

We looked at one another, she obviously a little startled at what she had said, then we both started to laugh.

It was the one bright spot in a long, dark day.

16 DIANE

Diane was an extremely attractive girl of sixteen. She was highly intelligent and mature and looked much older than her years. When I met her shortly after she had been admitted from court she was beautifully dressed. The clothes she wore were obviously expensive, as were her handbag and shoes. I'd never seen a girl like this before.

'What have you been doing to get yourself here?' I asked.

'Don't you know?' she asked.

'No.'

'Passing dud cheques.'

I noticed that she wore a beautiful wrist-watch.

'Have you? Cheque or cheques?'

'Cheques.'

'How many?'

'Oh, a great many. About three thousand quids' worth.'

I looked at her. I must have looked rather startled and she half smiled at me.

'How long have you been doing that?'

'Oh, for a long time.'

'What do you think is going to happen to you now?'

'I don't know.'

'Is this the first time you have been before the court?'

'No,' she said. 'I've been before the court four times before and . . . well . . . I've been in a couple of approved schools. I

103

suppose I'll get sent to Borstal now. Is it all right if I write to my grandmother?'

'Yes,' I said. 'Why? Do you live with her?'

'Yes, I live with my grandmother and she'll be upset.'

'Well, you write to her later.'

'Thank you,' she said and went off.

Later that night I was talking to her and she told me about the approved schools she had been in and from which she had absconded on many occasions. She talked about the headmistress of one of them with great affection.

'You obviously liked her,' I said.

'Yes, she was kind to me.'

'Why didn't you stay there?'

'I don't know. I suppose people like me will abuse kindness sooner or later.'

'You have a very low opinion of yourself.'

'Yes,' she said.

I got to know Diane very well during the weeks that followed. Her grandmother visited and it was obvious that they were very fond of one another.

Diane asked me one day if I could talk to her.

'Sure,' I said, and she came to my office.

'Do you know,' she said, 'when I was twelve I met a man.'

'Yes?'

'And he ran a brothel up near Clapham Common.'

'Yes?'

'I went to work there after school.'

'Did you?' I said.

'Yes. I should have hated it and tell you how terrible it was, but I can't really.'

'Why?'

'I had some good times there – does that sound terrible? Can you understand?'

'I think so.'

'Yes, well . . . the majority of people I got to know around there were bent.'

'They were?'

'Yes. Then last year, you know, I got to know stacks of them,' and she mentioned the name of a man who had not long previously received a very long sentence.

'Do you know him?'

'Yes, I know him. I was his girl friend for a long time.'

'But you are only sixteen now!'

'Yes, I know, but . . . well, I look older, don't I?'

'Yes, I suppose you do.'

'He's one of the top ones, you know.'

'You talk as if there is a hierarchy or a sort of class distinction among the criminal fraternity.'

'You bet there is,' she said. 'I know pubs and clubs where if some petty thief went in they'd sling him out. They've all got money and they have a sort of standard of manners and behaviour,' and she laughed. 'You think I'm pulling your leg, don't you?'

'I don't know really.'

'I'm not. It's a fact. I've worked in the clubs, too.'

I remembered seeing her deal a pack of cards and making it do everything except sit up and beg.

'Sometimes,' she said, 'when I'm sitting on a bus and I look at the people around me, I think, if they only knew about me they wouldn't sit next to me, they'd get up and go away if they'd known what I was doing when I was twelve.'

'What makes you think they would do that?'

'Because they are respectable people and, well, I'm not, am I?'

'But you're saying it. I don't know. Aren't you?'

'No, not really.'

'What do you want to do?' I asked.

'I'd like to be straight really, but I don't suppose I ever will be.'

'Why not?'

'Well, the only people I know are bent, Mr Hart.'

'What would you like to do, though?'

'I don't know. I'd like to work in a hotel or do something in catering. I think I could do well at that, but I don't suppose it will ever happen,' she said. 'They're sure to send me down the next time I go up.'

Diane was an extremely likeable girl and all the other girls looked to her for leadership. If she had wanted to she could have led them into a riot, but she never did. She was always telling them to behave themselves and not get into trouble.

She pointed out one girl to me. 'You see that girl over there?'

'Which one?'

She pointed her out. 'You know, she has a mother who writes to her and a father who comes to see her and they tell her to behave herself and all she wants to do is to go up bloody West. She wants her head examining.'

'Why don't you tell her so?'

'I have done. They eat girls like her up there. Somebody would put her on the game or get her pregnant . . . it's too stupid for words. If I had someone who wanted me like that, I'd go home.'

'What about your grandmother?'

'Yes, well . . . I don't half hurt her,' she said. 'Do you know she still goes out office-cleaning at six o'clock in the morning?'

'Well, if she loves you, why . . . ?'

'Yes, but that's different.'

'What's different?'

'She's got a family, that girl, and she ignores them. It's bloody stupid.'

Diane was seen by the psychiatrist and a probation officer came to see her. Reports were written and a plea was made for her to continue on probation. I waited to see what would happen at the court, and eventually was told that she was not coming back. We were all pleased and felt that if only she could be got away from her old friends she would be able to achieve some of the things she had talked about.

Some weeks went by and we were asked by the police to admit a girl who was being charged with non-payment of a meal in a restaurant. She had got up, walked out and been stopped outside. The name was not one I knew, but, when I walked down into the hall, it was Diane.

'Hello,' I said.

The police gave me the paper and I looked at Diane. 'This isn't your name. Your surname.'

'Yes, it is,' she said.

She sat in the office and I said, 'What about your name?'

'I got married.'

'You what?' I said.

'I got married.'

'Married?'

'Yes. Well, I met him again, I'd known him for some time and he's straight. He's in the army and he said he'd like to marry me.

106

I didn't believe anyone would ever want to marry me, so I agreed. I didn't believe him when we were at the Registry Office and I didn't believe him really after we were married.'

'But you got married?'

'Yes, I did.'

'Where is he now?'

'I don't know.'

'Why not?'

'Well, I left him the day after we got married.'

'Why did you do that?' I asked.

'I didn't love him. I didn't want to marry him really, I just didn't believe that anyone could ever want to marry me. I thought he was . . . well, I thought he was fooling me.'

'What are we going to do with you?' I asked.

'I don't know. This time they really will send me down.'

I looked at her, and this time she really did look thoroughly depressed. 'Hadn't you any money?'

'Yes,' she said. 'I had money when I walked out.'

'Then why did you do it?'

'Don't know, really. I ordered the most expensive thing on the menu and then I sneaked out, but they saw me.'

She seemed so depressed that she was seen by the psychiatrist again.

'Do you feel depressed?'

'Yes,' she said. 'I have felt like this before, you know. Whenever I'm depressed I do something stupid like pass a dud cheque or walk out without paying. What a waste.'

'Why?'

'Well, I gave away all the things I got with the dud cheques the last time. Do you know I once got a beautiful Rolex watch on a cheque, and do you know what I did with it?'

'No.'

'I put it down a drain.'

Once again, reports were prepared for the court. Everybody, including the probation officer, felt that it would be Borstal this time. Yet, in a way, we felt that this girl could still be helped. I suppose this was partly due to her personality, the fact that she was an extremely nice person, and the things that had happened to her as a child – maybe these things all contributed to the way everybody felt about her. The fact that she had no self-pity, didn't blame anybody else for the fact that she was in trouble with the law and made no attempt to justify it.

The psychiatrist arranged for her to be admitted to a psychiatric hospital's unit for young women, and the court accepted this placement. For twelve months Diane stayed there and went out to work. She got herself a job with a well-known firm of caterers and trained as an assistant manageress, then subsequently went to work in one of their restaurants.

She is now remarried and has a child and has emigrated. She still gets depressed, and on one occasion very nearly passed some more dud cheques. She is constantly surprised that the man she married should love her; she worships her baby and constantly worries in case 'she has my bad blood'.

'I shall always have doubts.'

'Doubts about what?' I asked her the last time I saw her.

'Whether anyone can really care for me.'

'Why don't you just accept it? Why don't you just accept that what's past is past? Look back on it and say, "It's over." '

'How can I say that when, in a sense, I know that I soiled myself from the age of twelve?'

'But you've had many a spring-clean since then,' I said.

She laughed. 'Yes, yes,' she said, 'but you know spring is a beautiful time.'

'Yes, it is.'

'Spring should be when you are about twelve. I don't think I ever knew spring.'

17 SARAH

I met Sarah during one of the visits I made to the United States. I noticed her the moment I entered the home in which she lived. She was like a picture advertising some American beauty preparation – tall and slim with a faint air of sophistication, but at the same time the freckles across her nose gave her a look of having lived outdoors. She gave the impression of being the all-American girl, if there is such a counterpart to the all-American boy. That faint air of upper-class breeding made her stand out from both staff and girls like a thoroughbred pony in a field of cart-horses.

She first talked to me one evening as we sat down to a meal.

'You've come from England, Mr Hart?'

'Yes. I thought that might be obvious.'

'I don't know, you haven't got one of those . . .' and she laughed deep within herself . . . 'well, you know what I mean.'

'No, I don't. You tell me.'

'Well, you know, one of those, um, snooty accents, I suppose. Yes, yes, that's right.'

'I'm from the North of England,' I said, 'and up there we don't need the affectation.'

'Well,' she said, 'none of us here come from Boston.'

The other girls laughed and I took it that Boston indicated having something like an Oxford English or BBC English accent. A kind of superiority. She asked me about where I lived in London

and about my family and my job and I found myself answering
her quite naturally, telling her things about myself and my family,
things about which I might normally have been more reticent.

'How old are you, Sarah?' I asked.

'Seventeen.'

It was warm that evening, and we sat outside with our backs
comfortably against a wall, looking out over very pleasant
countryside.

'I've been here two years,' she said, volunteering the information.

'Do you like it?'

'Yeah, yeah I do.'

'How did it start?'

'Do you mean what did I come for?'

'Yes, well . . . yes.'

'Well, I was incorrigible. Yes, I was taken to court because I
was incorrigible.'

I sat quietly, without speaking.

'Yeah, I was in a children's home,' she went on.

'How long were you there?'

'I guess since I was about thirteen, yeah, about . . . just before
I was thirteen,' she said, holding a blade of grass in her hand and
pushing it round and round. 'I'll tell you what, we could go up
to the house and . . . I don't know, perhaps I'll make you some
coffee. Would you like some coffee?'

I nodded.

We walked slowly up to the house and I sat alone in front of
the dining-room window until Sarah came back a few minutes
later with another girl.

'Do you know Molly?' she asked, and the young, black
American girl held out her hand.

'Hi!' she said.

They had brought a tray with them with three beakers of coffee
on it. We sat quietly drinking the coffee and the fact that we were
silent didn't seem to make any of us feel uncomfortable. We just
sat, rather content with the silence. Then they got up and took
the beakers away and I went up to my room to finish writing a
letter home. When I had finished I took it down to the sitting-
room where some of the girls were watching television. Through
in another room I could see more girls doing one another's hair.

110

'What are you doing?' asked Sarah coming over to me.

'I just wondered if there was somewhere I could leave this. I want to post it air-mail.'

'You ask Miss X if she'll put it in the post-box tomorrow morning, Mr Hart. Just mark it *air mail* and leave the money on the table in the office,' she said.

During the next few days Sarah would inevitably come and sit at my table for meals.

'You're getting on well with Sarah,' remarked a member of staff. 'She's not usually so pleasant . . . well, she's pleasant, but she doesn't usually have much to say.'

'Why is she here?'

'Maybe she will tell you. If not, I will.'

I remember that it was very late on the Saturday night and we were watching a film on television.

'Do you want some coffee, Mr Hart?'

I nodded.

'It's in the kitchen.'

I walked through into the kitchen where both Molly and Sarah were sitting.

'Do you like it here, Mr Hart?' Molly asked.

'Yes, I do.'

'Do you really?'

'Yes, I've enjoyed myself.'

'Why is that?'

'Well, everybody has been so nice to me.' They both looked pleased. 'Why, didn't you expect me to like it here?' Neither of them answered.

'I've been here twelve months,' said Molly. 'Not as long as Sarah, but gee, have I given them grief!'

'Why? Have you been difficult?' I asked.

She nodded her head as she stirred her coffee. 'I'm here for the same as Sarah, well . . . almost.'

The member of staff I'd spoken to earlier stood in the doorway. 'Hi!' she said.

'Hi yourself,' said Sarah.

'How about a cup of coffee? Or aren't we allowed in now that you've got Lord Hart?'

They all laughed.

'Sure.'

111

Sarah got up and poured out a beaker of coffee and put it on the table.

'I was going to tell Mr Hart why I am here.'

'Go on,' said the member of staff. 'Don't let me stop you. Would you rather I went?'

'No, not really.'

'Is it important for you to tell Mr Hart?'

Sarah looked across the table at her. 'Yeah, I guess so.'

'Why?'

'Well, he's a man and I've never talked to a man about it.'

'And Mr Hart will soon be 3,000 miles away, is that it?'

'Yeah, I guess so . . . but then I like him too.'

I was rather pleased and flattered and I felt that she meant it. It subsequently turned out that she did.

'Well, before we came to this part of the country,' she said, 'I lived at home with my mum and dad and my younger sister. We had a nice house and it was a nice part of the town we lived in. You know where I came from, don't you, miss?' she said, turning to the member of staff.

'Yes, but he'll believe you, you don't have to prove anything you say.'

The girl nodded.

Molly sat stirring her coffee. The noise from the other room filtered through and I could hear other girls laughing. She got up and shut the door.

'One day my mum was out,' said Sarah. 'I'd be about twelve and my father . . . I was very fond of my father, I loved him. Well, he came up to my room and he stood behind me and was stroking my hair, and then his hand went down on to my back, then he picked me up and laid me on the bed.'

She stopped and stared into the coffee as if she could see a picture there. None of us spoke. The member of staff sat in her chair looking across the table at Sarah. The silence seemed to last a long time. 'Well, I sure didn't know what he was doing. I'd just . . . well, at school I'd heard about things, but . . . well, then he told me not to tell my mother.'

'Why, because he'd been petting?'

She looked up from her coffee. 'Petting me nothing. He laid me, the bastard.' She was quiet again.

'Well, it went on for a long time after that – sometimes he'd take me in the car and other times we'd go up to the . . . well, you know, when my mother was out.'

'You never told her?'

'How could you tell your mother that was happening? Then I . . . well, after a time I didn't want to tell her. I don't suppose you could understand that, could you?'

'Yes, I think so,' I said.

Molly got up from her chair and picked up all the beakers of now cold coffee. She went across and put them down near the washing-up machine and brought over four more beakers which she topped up with coffee, then set them on the table.

'Well, when I was fourteen my father . . . my sister was two years younger than me.'

'Yes.'

'Well, I knew he'd begun to mess around with my sister and I . . . well, I told the police.'

'What happened?'

'Well, they arrested my father and everybody said how brave I'd been not to tell my mother, and how good I'd been to make sure the same kind of thing didn't happen to my sister . . . but it wasn't like that. It wasn't like that at all.'

She sat looking at me, but I had the feeling that she didn't see me.

'Do you know what it was like, Mr Hart?' she said.

I shook my head.

'I was jealous of the son of a bitch. Yeah, I was jealous. I didn't want him having my sister. Well, he went to prison and I was in bed one night when my mother came into my room. She was screaming and shouting and she had a strap in her hand. It was a belt off my father's pants and she began to hit me with it; the buckle cut me and I put up my arms to stop it hitting my face and she hit me and hit me and screamed at me. She said I was a lying bitch, that my father hadn't done the things I'd said he had and that she would kill me. I ran out on to the porch and she followed me, still screaming and shouting. I was in the yard when she suddenly said, "You killed him, you've killed him, you lying bitch!" '

Her voice had risen to a screech and I could hear the difference in her voice, as if she were imitating her mother's accent and tone.

'Well, he hung himself. Lots of people said I was lying and

113

some of the police tried to make me say . . . well, that I wasn't a virgin and that I'd been with other boys, but I wouldn't say it because it wasn't true. All I could think about was that I had killed my father . . . seems funny, well, not funny, strange, I guess,' she went on. 'Even when he was having me, afterwards I still thought of him as my father, you know. I still wanted him to get me candy and things. Well, then I went to a children's home up state. It was all right up there, I went to school there and it was pretty good. I used to think about my father though, and I'd be so frightened. I was frightened,' she said, answering her own question, 'because I knew I'd really . . . well, I had killed him. If I hadn't said anything he'd still have been there.

'Then one day I was in the house when one of the kids who was older than I was came in and said, "Sarah was having it with her father you know". Well, I hit her, gee, I really did hit her. I had a cup in my hand and I just let her have the lot. There was blood all over the place. I went to the court and then I went up to Juvenile Hall where they had a psychiatrist. I told him what the girl had said but I didn't tell him anything else. But anyway, the girl I'd hit admitted that she'd said it. I had to go back to the home, but by this time it was all around the school why the girl had had twenty stitches in her head. They all talked about me, but didn't want to talk to me, the girls I mean. I used to . . . well I used to go with some of the fellers and they'd try to get me to . . . but I didn't.

'Then I was on my way home from school one day when I met one of the boys from our class and I stopped to talk to him. His elder brother came up. I liked him, he was about eighteen, I guess, and he asked would I like to go out with him . . . well, he wanted to date me and I said "Yes". He took me out and we had a drink and well, I didn't say "No" to him. It went on for some weeks and then one night he said would I like to go to a party. I said I would have difficulty in getting permission from the home, but he said, "Well, come anyway", so I went.

'I went to this party – there were some other girls and they all said, "Well, she's used to it." There were seven fellers and they all screwed me – they all thought it was a great joke, so did the other girls who stood around watching. There was some booze and I drank a lot. What had happened soon went round the school and people began to ask me if it was true, but I denied it and so did the other girls and the fellers. Well, they'd have gone to prison too, and though I hated their guts, I couldn't forget how I'd killed my father.

'After that I used to get the fellers to bring me booze and they could have what they wanted. I couldn't sleep at night so I used to take the booze and hide it in the garden, then I used to drink it and take some aspirin. In the end I ran away. I always looked older than my age and I met a feller and . . . this guy, I lived with him. Then one day I was picked up and I was drunk. Yeah – yeah, I was drunk. I was drinking nearly a bottle of the stuff a day.'

I looked towards the member of staff, who inclined her head slightly.

'Yes, that was it I guess,' she said.

'Well, then I went back to Juvenile Hall and . . . it was terrible – all I wanted to do was to run away and get a drink. I managed to do it once and when they picked me up I really was drunk. I really mean that . . . drunk. If you spread your drinks out over the day, late afternoon and evening, you can get pretty high, you can get a glow and, well, you can be very drunk. When you get like that you don't have to think. When I was sober I couldn't sleep at all – all I could think of was my father and then being banged up by seven guys while a shower of shitty females looked on. Then I came here. I haven't done too badly.'

She stood up slowly and stretched as if she were waking from a dream. Slowly she sat back down in her chair and put both hands round the coffee beaker, then made a face when she found how cold it was. Molly got up and took away the four cups, then came back with another four.

'Why did you have to tell Mr Hart?'

'I don't know, really.'

'Yes, you do.'

'Thought he might understand and he's going to be too far away to tell anyone.'

The two girls stood up. 'You haven't said anything,' Sarah said to me.

'I don't know what to say, except that I feel very proud and very humble that you told me. Nothing I could say would make it any better, would it?'

Sarah shook her blonde hair. 'You're too right.'

"Night, miss.'

They kissed the member of staff and walked to the door then, as an afterthought, they turned back, both of them, and kissed me on the cheek.

'Good night.'

'Good night,' I said.

I looked at the clock on the wall – it was four o'clock in the morning. Time seemed to have passed, yet I couldn't realize that we had been sitting there for over three and a half hours.

'You are very honoured,' said the staff member.

'Yes, I suppose I am,' I said.

'You truly are. We've been trying to get her to talk like this for two years. Maybe it just needed a stranger, someone . . .'

'Yes, I think you're right.'

The staff member went out through the door and I suddenly realized that she was crying.

After I came home I heard from Sarah occasionally and I heard about her from some of the staff. She was doing well in her job, a good job she had in a hospital. She kept in touch with the member of staff. The rest of the story was told to me by that member of staff in a letter she sent me . . .

Sarah was then getting on for twenty. She continued to do well in her job and she was sharing an apartment with two other girls from the hospital. She had been dating a young man for about twelve months and had told him she was an orphan. She had not told him about the institution she had been in.

One week-end she turned up there. 'You know, miss,' she said to the social worker who had sat with me and heard her story, 'he wants to marry me.'

'Gee, that's great.'

'Yeah. Says he loves me.'

'Well, that's great, too.'

'Yeah – but do I tell him? Do I tell him about my father? I know I don't have to tell him about the other fellers, but he might find out about you and, well, I wouldn't want . . .'

'He wouldn't really have to know at all.'

'Yeah, I know that but . . .'

'What do you want to do?'

She said that Sarah sat for a long time then said, 'Well, I guess I'll tell him. Do you think that if he loves me, really loves me, it will make any difference, miss?'

'Well, it shouldn't, but I don't know,' said the social worker. 'Have you been . . . ?'

Sarah shook her head. 'No, we haven't had sex,' she said. 'There's been no other guy.'

My friend drove her back to the town and went back to the home, but by the week-end she began to feel worried, though she wasn't sure why; however, she drove back into the town and to Sarah's apartment. The door was opened by the girls who shared the apartment with Sarah.

'Come in,' they said.

My friend said it looked as though a battleship had gone through the place. Things were smashed and Sarah was so drunk that she looked as if she were dead as she lay on the floor. She told the girls to call an ambulance and when it arrived Sarah was picked up and taken to hospital.

'How much has she been drinking?'

'She didn't come back until the day before yesterday,' said one of the girls. They found nine big, empty Bourbon bottles.

Sarah remained unconscious for some time before she gradually began to recover, but, according to the social worker, she looked as if she were about fifty years old.

'I told him. He said he was sorry but his love didn't extend as far as condoning that kind of behaviour.'

'So what did you do?'

'I told him the rest and I called him a S.O.B.'

'Why did you go back to drinking?'

'I was coming to see you, miss,' she said, 'but well, I didn't. I guess I've lost my job now. I don't know.'

'Come and stay with us for a while. You could stay in my apartment at the institution.'

Sarah nodded, and a week later went out to stay with the social worker.

'You don't have to worry about me drinking.'

My friend did worry, but Sarah didn't drink. The hospital transferred her to another section from where she went backwards and forwards to work. Then she met a young man. He was a regular guy, had a good job and was going to evening classes. He asked Sarah out and my friend encouraged her to go. It was like a real old-fashioned courtship and they used to sit on the steps outside the apartment door to talk. If she was going to be late back, they would phone to let the social worker know.

Then, one day, as she was sitting in the kitchen, the young man came in. 'Do you think Sarah would marry me if I asked her?'

She said she felt like saying, 'Oh my God, not that all over again,' but just said, 'Well, you could ask her.'

She said he must have seen the look in her eyes for he answered, 'I know all about Sarah, I know all about her old man and the other guys.'

'Doesn't it matter?'

'Of course it matters,' he said, 'I would like to . . .' But what he would have liked to have done is not printable.

'When are you thinking of getting married if she says yes?'

'I'll need a bit of time to pass these exams and then to get a better job.'

'Yes, I reckon you will.'

Then I had a letter from Sarah. How would I like to go to the United States and give her away? 'Gee, it would be great to see you,' she wrote.

I wrote back to congratulate her.

Then one night as I was sitting at home the phone rang; it was my friend the social worker.

'Hi, Tom,' she said.

'Hello. Is something wrong?' Something in her voice made me feel apprehensive.

'Yes. Sarah.'

'What's the matter with her?'

'She's in hospital.'

'What's wrong?'

'Well, she's got leukaemia, and though she doesn't know it, she isn't going to get better. She's coming home tomorrow for a few days.'

'Home?'

'Yes, here,' she said, 'to the apartment. I said she could phone you and tell you herself.'

'Tell me what?'

'She's going to get married.'

'Does he know?'

'Yes, he knows.'

I waited for the phone call the next day.

'Hi, Mr Hart.'

118

'Hello, Sarah.'

'You heard?'

'Yes, you've been in hospital. Are you feeling better?'

'Yeah. I'm feeling fine.'

'When are you getting married?'

'Saturday. Will you think of us?'

'I'll be thinking of you. I wish I could be there.'

'Yes. I wish you could. I've told John all about you. Would you like to speak to him?'

I said I would and we spoke for a few minutes before Sarah came back on the phone. 'Good night. Good night, Mr Hart,' she said.

'Good night and God bless you, Sarah,' I said. 'I hope you'll be very happy.'

I had a card and then a letter telling me all about the wedding and who had been there; all her friends and the girls at work and John's relatives – apparently his parents were dead.

Then I received this letter:

Dear Mr Hart,

I am writing to tell you how happy I am now and how happy I have been over these last few weeks. Miss X has been such a good friend to me and I love her very much. John has been so good and kind. I don't think John knows what is happening to me. I told the doctor not to tell him or Miss X but I thought that as you were so far away I could tell you and share a secret which is a heavy burden, and I know they will be in touch with you when it is all over. I have been so happy and I love him so much and I am happy too because when I think of all the things I have done, all the wrong things, God must have forgiven me by giving me such happiness, such love as John and Miss X have given me and your friendship. Think of me and remember that I love you.

Sarah

Sarah died four weeks later. She deserved more happiness and more love than she received, but doubtless the love she had for such a short span burned bright and fierce and never dimmed. It says much for the human spirit that it can rise above such handicaps.

119

18 JACKIE

It was quite late at night when the new girl was admitted. She was indescribably dirty, verminous, extremely tired and hungry. When all her physical needs had been met she went to bed. The following day she joined the group in which she was going to live.

'Hey, Mr 'Art,' said Jackie when I went into the room, 'she's an odd one, that girl.'

'Why, what makes you say that?'

'Well, as soon as she came into the group she told us she wanted us to understand that she were the boss.'

'Oh, of where?'

'Of the group.'

'What did you say, Jackie?'

'Well, I dropped a curtsy like and said that if she got funny I'd give her a mouthful of knuckle.'

'That wasn't a very ladylike thing to say.'

'Well, she weren't very ladylike herself.'

Suddenly I heard the new girl, in a voice loud enough for me to hear, ask another girl, 'Who's the bloody geezer with the pipe?'

'That's Mr Hart.'

'What's he?'

'He runs the place.'

'What's he like?'

'He's not bad, he's all right . . . well, sometimes.'

'Oh. He bosses you around does he?'

'Sometimes.'

'Oh. Bleeding well not better start on me,' she said.

The sitting-room went quiet and the girls all turned their eyes in my direction.

'What did I tell you?' said Jackie.

'I heard it.'

'Yeah, well, there's one everywhere,' she said.

I went over to the new girl.

'Well, what's the matter with you?' I asked.

'Fuck off.'

'You know, people here try to be polite to one another,' I said.

'You know what you are?'

I looked at her not wishing to say 'No' in case she told me.

'I know who I am, and I think perhaps you'd better come along with me,' I said. 'We'll have a talk.'

'You're a bloody fat pig of a bastard.'

'Are you coming with me?' I asked.

'I'll come with you, mate,' she said. 'See if I care.' She followed me out of the room and we walked down to one of the offices.

'What was all that about?' I asked her.

Without another word she burst into tears. She covered her face with her hands and sobbed. I thought this girl was one who could be better dealt with by my wife, so I called her and she came in.

She turned out to be a very angry and deprived girl who was totally unable to make friends and whose opinion of herself was so low as to be almost non-existent. The only way she could impress was by her toughness, but, unfortunately, she was not very tough. I went back to the sitting-room.

'Where is she?' asked Jackie.

'Talking to Mrs Hart,' I said.

'Yeah. That must have upset you, what she called you.'

'Well, not all that much; she was angry,' I said.

'I don't mean the bastard bit.'

'No?'

'No, I mean the fat pig bit – you certainly are putting it on, Mr 'Art.'

'Jackie,' I said, 'I know when she's being difficult and I know when she's being cheeky, but I'm not quite sure about you.'

'I'm just one of nature's wits, sir,' she said. 'Night night.'

I never saw Jackie again after she left us. I hope she did well. The other little girl went to a school, stayed in the same district when she left the school and married a local boy. She takes her baby to school to see the staff. She deserved happiness and I understand that she found it.

19 FRANCES

I saw Frances standing in the front hall one Sunday morning at about ten o'clock. She was wearing a fur cape and a long, sheath-like evening gown. The gown was split up one side to half-way between her knee and her hip.

'Where have you come from?' I asked.

'They picked me up in a club last night,' she said.

'You look tired.'

'I am tired.'

Her eyelashes were so long that when she fluttered them I imagined I felt a breeze go by my ear. Her make-up, which was somewhat in disarray, had obviously been put on originally with considerable skill. She looked about twenty-two years of age, standing there in this dress and her high-heeled shoes.

I looked at the form the police had brought with her. Her age was down as fifteen years and one month. It said that she had been missing from home for four months. She sat in my office while I explained that she would be going to court.

'Yes, so I understand.'

She was said to be in need of care or protection and in moral danger.

'You go on Tuesday,' I said. 'You look tired. Would you like to have a bath and go to bed?'

'Yes,' she said, 'I didn't get much sleep in the police station.'

One of the staff took her off to get her bath.

'You know the dress that girl was wearing?' she said to me later that morning.

'Yes.'

'That was all she had on . . . in the middle of winter.'

'She must have felt cold.'

'You're not kidding.'

Frances told me that she earned her living as a stripper in the clubs. She had £60 in her handbag.

'Did you earn that stripping?'

'Mmm,' she said, 'I earn more than that.'

'How much can you earn?'

'Well, if you work hard I suppose what you could earn is practically unlimited, but I used to earn about £100 a week.'

'Just in one club?'

'No. You go round the clubs, you know, each day. You sort of do a strip here and a strip there.'

'What are the clubs like?' I asked.

'You mean the ones I go to? They're pretty tatty, you know, and they charge terrible prices and the hostesses rook you as well.'

'What made you take up this profession?'

'I used to go up West on Saturday nights.'

'Did your parents know?'

'Yes, they knew, and I used to say I stayed up there because I couldn't get back. I used to stay down . . .' and she mentioned the name of a club . . . 'and a fellow saw me there and said, "How about going on the game?"'

'How old were you then?'

'Fourteen.'

'What did you say?'

'I said, "no thank you".'

'Then what happened?'

'Well, I met a girl who was stripping. She was in here once,' and she mentioned the girl's name. 'She's eighteen now, and she took me to her flat and said, "I bet you have the figure for stripping," and she had a look and said I had.'

I looked at this slim, rather well-proportioned girl.

'They like them like me,' she said, 'in stripping. Well, I'm tall, and in a little gym slip and panama hat it turns them on.'

'Who got you the job then?'

'Oh, my friend did.'

'Did they know your age?'

'Well, yes, they did really, but they pretended they didn't, you know.'

She looked much younger with her make-up off and her hair tied back in a pony-tail.

'Why did you go away from home. Don't you like your parents?'

'Yes. They were very good to me, my parents. I don't know, I like it up there, I like the life and we can look after ourselves, my friend and I.' She looked at me. 'I wouldn't go on the game,' she said.

'Nevertheless,' I said, 'there could be certain consequences, you could end up pregnant.'

'Yes. I suppose so, but I'm careful and I don't go in for that much anyway. You see, my friend's a Les.'

She told me about the clubs and how she would do her act, if that is the name for it, first at one club and then go on to another and another. Apparently she got so much from each club she performed in.

She was talking to the girls and staff one night.

'What time do you start, Fran?' asked one girl.

'One place opens up so early you can get a show in there just after nine o'clock.'

'And have you done that?'

'Yeah, I started doing it at that time, you know. You want to see them in there . . . all the men.' She said 'men' with such disdain, almost distaste. 'They sit there, nine o'clock in the morning, watching girls take their knickers off.'

'Are they old men?' asked one girl.

'No, not all of them. A lot of them are about your age,' she said pointing, to me. She smiled. 'Didn't mean anything by that,' she said, 'but you know what I mean, about your age.'

'Yes, I know what you mean.'

'But you get a lot of young fellows there too, standing around, but the old men just sit watching you. And nine o'clock in the morning, well, you don't feel much like it,' she said. 'You just walk on and, well, you just take them off, you've no interest really. You look at them out there and they make you feel sick.'

'Who do?' asked a girl.

'The men do. They're bleeding useless as men. They sit there and you can imagine them wanting to paw you and I suppose they

127

do. It's different at night when the place has warmed up and, well, there's a bit more noise and a bit more life.'

'Do they just pay for one show?'

'No. They can sit there all bleeding night if they want. They're all pretty useless.'

'How do you mean, useless?'

'Well, they're useless as men, aren't they? They don't go out and pick up floosies on the street, you know.'

'Why not?'

'Well, cost them more, anyway,' and she looked at me. 'Well, they'd be no damned good there either, you know.'

'Don't you feel sorry for them?' asked a girl.

'Used to. I used to think what queer kind of wives they must have. I used to think that if their wives were well, better . . . you know what I mean?'

'No, what do you mean?'

'Well, maybe if their wives were more loving,' she said. 'Yes, that's it . . . more loving, maybe they wouldn't be up there watching girls. We used to go on in a morning and look at them and you'd take 'em off and twirl 'em round and stand for a split second then walk off. In a way, you know, you did it to insult 'em. But, as I say, it was better at night, but even then you didn't have much time for them, any of 'em. Some of them, you know, would wait outside for you to come out and offer you money if you'd go with them and strip for them. Chaps used to be around, you know, and ask if you'd pose for them for photographs.'

'Did you ever do that, Fran?'

'No, not me. Some girls earn quite good money at it. Do you know so and so?' she asked me. 'She earns a bomb at it.'

I realized that that particular girl was not yet sixteen. Frances was attractive and of average intelligence.

'Would you like to go home,' I asked, 'to your parents?'

'Yes, I think I would.'

'But would you go back up there, doing that?'

'I don't know. I think I've had enough, really. I enjoyed it to begin with, but after a time, you know, it becomes a chore,' she said. 'I like some of the people I met up there. Well, the queers were the best.'

'Why?'

'Well, they were nice to you. They'd talk to you without wanting anything out of you . . . lot of them up there, lot of foreigners, too, all they want to do is to ponce on you.' She thought for a while. 'Yes, I think I'd like to go home.'

Her parents turned out to be two ordinary, likeable people who had four other children, two older than Frances. They appeared, from all accounts, to be a pretty united family, not affluent but not in any financial difficulty either.

I was standing at the window of my office one morning and could see Frances in the play area with some of the staff and girls. She was standing against the wall bouncing a ball off the wall, jumping out and letting it pass between her legs. Another girl caught it and Frances would run to the end of the line, and so it went on. I saw her skipping and then playing tag as they ran around. One couldn't really reconcile the girl playing these games with the girl I'd seen admitted who had told about her experiences in the clubs.

Frances went to court and a supervision order was made, then she returned home. I never heard of Frances again, but her probation officer said, when I once asked, 'Yes, she's doing all right. She's settled down at home. She's an odd girl. In a way you'd think she'd never been away from home.'

Perhaps Frances had seen enough and learnt enough of that world to last her a lifetime, but I often wonder what the man was like – if there was a man – what the man was like whom she eventually married.

20 ELLA

'Are you afraid of dying, Mr Hart?'

Ella sat quietly in a chair opposite me. She sat with her hands folded in her lap. She was a beautiful girl with hair that shone like polished brass. Her eyes were grey, her face was oval and she had long, well-shaped hands. She could sit almost motionless, her eyes never leaving your face. She talked with an intensity one wouldn't expect to find in a girl of fifteen.

'I don't know about dying. I suppose it's a subject the majority of people don't give a lot of thought to and I suppose I'm one of those. If I do think about it I suppose I find death . . . well . . . unreal and a long way off and, in any case, I have no particular wish to die. Why do you ask?'

'I often think of death. Not as something I should be afraid of but, in a way, to prepare myself for.'

'How do you mean, prepare yourself?'

'Well, learn to see it as something pleasant and not unpleasant. As if it were going to be . . . I suppose as if I were going to visit a country I can only imagine. Where it will be, well, peaceful.'

'Why, don't you find anything peaceful?'

'No.'

'Why not?'

'I've been to too many places and found them all . . . well, very frightening.'

'In what way have you found them frightening?'

131

'Well, I have always been a stranger there. Never found anywhere I was part of, or belonged to, if you know what I mean.'

'Why?'

'Because the people there didn't want me particularly.'

'Do you think that's true, or could it be just you? Maybe the fault wasn't always with the others.'

'No, I don't think it was, but in a way they wanted me to pretend. Everybody wants you to pretend when you are like us.'

'How do you mean, like us?'

'Well, like the majority of the people here.'

'In what way do you think we want you to pretend?'

'You want us to pretend that we are happy. People want us to pretend that we like them ... well ... when we don't. And agree with them when we don't. You can't be yourself, you've always got to be what other people want you to be – you've always got to see what they see.'

'You could be making excuses for your own inability to make relationships. Perhaps you are looking for excuses for whatever has gone wrong in the past. Maybe you are projecting your unhappiness on to other people without justification.'

Ella sat and thought, again perfectly still, her eyes looking past me and through me. I lit my pipe and waited for her to speak.

'I suppose if you didn't have some excuse,' she said, 'some reason for your unhappiness, what would be the point of living? Perhaps we are seeking the truth about what is happening to us.'

'Do you think the truth is always good? Do you think we are always ready to know the truth about ourselves?'

'I think we should always know the truth about our relations, our parents .... when you think of it, they are not dead to you, but you are dead to them. It seems they never wanted you. My parents, my real parents, I don't know about them, do I? Nobody will tell me about them. My adopted parents, they are nice people and they say they love me.'

'And don't you think they do?'

'Yes, I suppose they did but they can't really love you because they don't understand. All I wanted to know was who I am, what I am and where I came from, but when I asked they were angry.'

'Maybe they were just upset. Maybe they were afraid of losing you.'

'Why should they be afraid of that? Why should they be afraid

132

of talking about the truth? I never meet anybody who wants to tell me the truth. I searched for my mother.'

'Yes, I know.'

'People seem to think that was a stupid thing to do and when I went back home to my adopted parents they . . . they didn't want to know me. I suppose they think I had denied them something.'

'That's a strange thing to say.'

'What? Denied them?' she said. 'Well, maybe I did really, maybe I should have been content.'

'Are you regretting it now, that you were not content?'

'Yes, of course, but I couldn't be other than what I am, I can't change my feelings. You know, when I get depressed I do stupid things.'

'Such as what?'

'Well, I usually go to bed with someone.'

'Do you still feel depressed afterwards?'

'Yes. Not that I really care for them, but once I am depressed I care for them. I don't suppose people find it possible to understand . . . and then I run away from everywhere. Think of all the places I've been to.'

'How many places have you been to?'

'About twelve I suppose.'

'I'm sure people would help if you'd let them.'

'Why don't people let you talk?'

'I'm sure they would if you wanted to.'

'Not really, not like this anyway. They think it's adolescent nonsense and nobody has time to listen to that. Do you mind listening to adolescent nonsense?'

'I don't think you are talking nonsense particularly.'

'All the words and the feelings are inside you, you know, and we've nobody to tell them to. Have you ever walked through London in the middle of the night when you were cold and had nowhere to go?'

'No. I've never done that.'

'Well, if you do, supposing you are walking towards Fleet Street – there are those churches in the middle of the road, you know?'

'Yes, I know.'

'Well, at night when it's dark there seems to be a shadow and as you go by them, you feel cold, and when you get cold you suddenly feel afraid and you want to run. Then if you run you are afraid, because if some policeman sees you he will chase you, so you stand in a doorway and wait. If you don't hear anything you're afraid of stepping out of the doorway in case somebody is standing in the next doorway and perhaps he is going to jump out on you.'

'That's how you feel?'

She went on talking as if I hadn't interrupted her. 'You light a fag if you've got one and then you go on walking towards Fleet Street. Sometimes when you get there, there are people around, particularly near the newspaper offices. Sometimes the fellows who work on the papers – the men who work on the machines – they talk to you. Some of them are quite nice and you get a cup of tea and a bit of a warm-up. When you get to the top end see St Paul's under that bridge, that's a frightening place. You turn round and walk back up. I've walked up and down that street and never seen a policeman – other times you wonder where they all come from. When it's raining and you stand in the doorways, that's the worst.'

'Why?'

'The rain always seems to drive in and you have to get back in the corner and you feel cold and wet. Then, when you get really fed up, you go to the back of the Dilly to one of the clubs. It's dark and you can sit down. Some fellow will come up to you and if he doesn't want you to score [buy drugs] he'll talk to you and buy you a cup of coffee. Sometimes they ask you if you are on the run, and they'll offer you a bed if you say "yes". They'll offer you one if you say "no", anyway. You go out into Soho and it's always half light.

'Sometimes you can stand and see the lights over London. If you're in the right place outside. London's never dark and yet, because it isn't, in some way it's much darker. The doorways are dark and the shadows from the buildings are darker and when it's raining . . . it's like walking on glass, black glass. When a light shines on it it's lighter and you can see where you're going, but other times it's dark and frightening. In the day time the whole damn place is tatty. The Dilly's tatty, Soho's tatty . . . so scruffy and dirty and the blokes are tatty too. You feel it, you feel just the same as them, you know. It's like those buildings that are all front and nothing behind, they look all kind of imposing from one

134

side, all brightly lit up with neon lights . . . like the Coca-Cola sign . . . when it's lit up at night it's quite nice, isn't it, going on and off? But when you see it in the daytime it's dead and shabby.

'That's what it's like. It's all empty and has no meaning. It's sort of aimless. You're looking for something round there. You're looking for something beautiful really. Lean on the wall in Trafalgar Square and look up at the art gallery at the back when it's sunny in the summer . . . you can watch all the people on the balcony, all the tourists with their cameras, the Americans . . . and the Germans with their guide-books.'

'How do you tell one from another?'

'Oh, that's easy.'

'Why?'

'The Americans look at everything with a kind of sense of pleasure and awe and the Germans look at it as if they could have done better.'

'Don't you like the Germans?'

'Yes, I do, but, I don't know, they have a kind of air of disdain, you know.'

'The Americans don't?'

'No. Usually if you ask a young American for a couple of bob they'll give it to you. And they'll talk to you about London and ask you questions about yourself.' She tried to imitate an American. ' "*Where do you live, honey? What are you doing? Do you live in London?*" "I'm on the run." "*Where from?*" "An approved school." "*Gee, what's an approved school?*" Well, you tell them some tale about how terrible it is and why you are there and why you ran away. They're always sympathetic. If you ask a German, they just say *nein* or ignore you or push past you.'

'Who else is there?'

'The Australians. They're not so good either.'

'You don't like the Australians?'

'They're all right if you meet them in a club or at night, but not to try and touch them for a bob or two. People from up North are all right, you know. I worked for a chap, well not exactly worked . . . he used to do sketches of Trafalgar Square and places and I used to go round and try and flog them to the tourists. The people from up North usually bought, but the Americans didn't think much of art, it was easier to try and get something out of them for nothing than to try and sell them something . . . unless

you could tell them it was antique and well . . . my friend didn't
do anything that looked antique.'

'Was he any good at drawing?'

'Yes, he was really good.'

'Where is he now?'

'He's in the nick.'

'What for?'

'Being in possession.'

'Oh.'

'When all the tourists are here you are part of the scene, but
when they have gone and it's night-time again . . . one of the worst
places to walk down at night is Whitehall. Not that you do it very
often, there are too many policemen about. I used to go down there
with —— [she mentioned the name of another girl]. She weren't
very bright, you know.'

'No, I know.'

'She got nicked, you know.'

'What for?'

'Indecency.'

'What did she do . . . if you don't mind my asking?'

'She got undressed and had a wash in the fountain in Trafalgar
Square, about four o'clock in the morning. Didn't think anybody
would see her, but they did. They grabbed her, well, they didn't
actually grab her, they had to chase her half-way up Regent
Street. She was running like hell with her clothes in her hand trying
to put them on at the same time. It was a bit of a scream.'

'Did you see it?'

'Yes, I saw it, it was a bit of a scream, but it was all so bloody
pathetic really. All so pathetic. In some ways it made you feel . . .
well, degraded.'

'Then why do it?'

'Well there isn't anywhere else to go, is there? You don't belong
anywhere and you don't feel that you want to belong anywhere.
I'd like to belong, though.'

'Did you ever go back home?'

'Yes, after I had been in approved school, but my mum kept
saying "You let us down after all we did for you", and though
maybe she didn't mean it in the way it sounded, it was the "We
took you in and gave you a good home" bit and I couldn't stay
after that.'

'Didn't you love them?'

'Yes, I did, though nobody believes me now. I still couldn't go back, though.'

'Why, is it your pride that's hurt?'

'It's nothing to do with pride, really, it's the way you feel.'

'So what now?'

'They'll probably send me to another school.'

'And then what?'

'I don't know. I suppose they'll tell me I ought to get some "O"-levels or something.'

'That's not bad advice.'

'Who am I doing it for?'

'For yourself, for your own satisfaction.'

'Do you mean, do it for yourself and see what happens later on?'

'Something like that.'

'It doesn't make me much different from what I am now. I don't care, really.'

'From what you've told me about the life you've been leading, you don't appear to be particularly happy.'

'No, I'm not, but then I'm not particularly unhappy either, I just kind of exist. You just wait for each day and look at it.'

'Look at what?'

'Look at each day and the places and the people and hope that they'll change, but they don't.'

'Perhaps you need to change before everything else will change.'

'Yes. I suppose that's true. But what am I changing for? So that I'll belong somewhere?'

'Perhaps in the hope that you'll be happier.'

'But it won't be for me, will it? It will be for somebody else.'

'Perhaps one way to be happy is to make someone else happy.'

'Yes, but there is a difference between happiness and fun, happiness and laughter. Sometimes you have one big giggle and meet people and it's fun – it's all laughing and fun. When you try to think what you were happy about you don't know because there wasn't anything; just, for a time, you were happy with people and then they go off because they are just like you. Maybe we understand one another because we are in the same mess, because we haven't any future.'

'Don't you think you have a future?'

137

'Do you? Honestly? Tell me the truth.'

'In a way you have to create your own. You have some half-formed idea of what it is you want, and then you grope towards it, in a sense. I think everybody does that, Ella. Maybe there is no such thing as true happiness . . . you only get a little of it now and again.'

'But what if you feel there's nothing inside you? You're just a shell. Can you tell me what you do then?'

'No, I can't. Perhaps . . .'

'Perhaps what?'

I looked at her and was at a loss. I didn't know what to tell her. She sat quite still, her hands in her lap, and although her voice had sounded animated at times, she herself had never moved.

'I've seen more psychiatrists than . . . well, you know the saying . . . than I've had hot dinners, and they all tell me the same, that I have to sort out my own problems and that nobody can do it for me. I have to get rid of all the anger about my real mother.'

'Are you angry?'

'No, not really. I might be angry if I didn't feel so dead. Nothing seems to matter except that tonight comes and I have to live through it until the morning comes.'

'Is the night so bad?'

'No, only I feel more and see more at night when I'm outside. It's only then, in a sense, that I see the buildings and the churches and even old Nelson up there on his column; you look up and feel that if you just call out to him, any minute he'll jump. Daft, isn't it? At night you can make things seem any way you want to if you can shut out the cold and shut out the fear, but when the fear comes . . . then you really despise yourself. Wish to God you were a man.'

'Why?'

'You'd be taking someone else to bed and using them, not them using you. Maybe if you were a man you could find someone and love them.'

'Someone like you?'

'Yes, maybe. Maybe someone like me. Next day you get up and, "You're going to stay?" "Yes, I'll stay, give us ten bob to get some food in," and they give it to you and you blow.'

'Do you ever meet them again?'

'Sometimes, and sometimes they come over and ask you why you went and get a bit rough, but not often. You threaten to scream or tell the police. Anyway, what do they want for ten bob?'

'Why go to bed with them like that?'

'You shut your eyes and pretend it isn't happening. They tell you, you know, "Come on", and you want to spit in their eye. I suppose it's that I won't love and they want the illusion of love.'

'Illusion?' I asked.

'Yes, you know. They want to be kidded. I feel as if I've been kidded all my life, I feel I've had the illusion of love and it's not very nice.'

'Would you like to be loved?'

'Yes.'

'You will be if you give people a chance.'

'Give them a chance? You can't do that. You can't afford to do that.'

'Why not?'

'Give them a chance and they'll take advantage of you.'

'Not everybody.'

'Everybody I've known and the ones I haven't known. My mother, if she had given me a chance, I'd have loved her no matter what she did.'

She sat still, thinking again. 'I did love my adoptive parents. I still do. If they hadn't talked to me as if I'd been taken from the Battersea Dogs' Home and made me a member of the Puppy Club or whatever it's called.'

Ella went to another school, but she didn't stay. She was on the run again and I occasionally heard about her from other girls, then I heard that she was in Borstal. After that I heard no more, but I often remembered her conversation and I also kept some of her poetry. Occasionally I saw it in my drawer and took it out and read it for a few moments and wondered what had become of her, then I turned again to the immediate problems of my job, my own life, my hopes and desires in which Ella had no part.

21   THE VISIT

One day I was a member of a party visiting a special hospital, a party of doctors going to see the work that was done there. We arrived at the hospital, six of us, and were introduced to the consultant, who gave us coffee and talked about the work in the hospital. He talked of the problems of caring for so many men and women in a hospital which was so over-crowded and that had been built before the beginning of the century. Two retired male nurses took us on a tour of the hospital, including most impressive workshops where they made beautiful furniture. In one corner of the workshop was a young man with an easel and oils and his paintings were quite startling. I stood and talked to him.

'Do you like them?' he asked.

'Yes, very much,' I said. 'What do you do with them?'

'I sell them.'

'Did you learn to paint before you came here?'

'Yes, I did.'

We talked about his paintings and he asked me if I painted. I acknowledged that I tried.

'It's a frustrating business, isn't it?'

I acknowledged that too.

'When you start you've got to go on,' he said.

We talked for a while about the difficulty of putting on to canvas whatever it is you are trying to say. 'It makes me angry,'

I said. 'I feel I lack the talent to paint whatever it is I am trying to portray.'

'Yes, I know what you mean,' he said.

We talked for a little longer, and then I had to move on and he went back to his easel and his paint. Further along were men working with electrical components; they were repairing television sets. Another man was doing marquetry, and it was his ambition to reproduce the Bayeux Tapestry complete in marquetry. Each scene that he had completed was beautifully depicted in inlaid wood.

'It's going to take you a long time, isn't it?'

'It will take me x number of years and x number of months,' he said.

'What will you do with it when you finish it?'

'I shall send it home.'

His home had originally been abroad, and he said it was going to be put up there, either in the library or the school, he said, I can't remember which. Men were working with tools of all kinds, as in the tailor's shop, where they made clothes for each other and uniforms for the staff.

There was a community centre and I remember there was a notice on the board which said there was to be a concert on the Saturday evening and that the admission fee would be 1s. 6d. The money raised was to be used 'for the impoverished members of this parish'. I was shown the church and where the men lived. Some lived in what had been cells, but, with the money they had earned, or had perhaps been sent in, many had bought carpets and radios and other luxuries to make their lives more tolerable and give them a certain degree of privacy.

Others were in wards which appeared to be overcrowded. Much had been done by the authorities to make them more habitable, but one could imagine what it must be like to have to live in crowded conditions like this, with such an all-pervasive lack of privacy. Few appeared to have any complaints, though, and the majority talked of events within the hospital, although many appeared to be well informed about what was going on outside as well. Some of these men had been here for many years, and some knew they might never go out.

The hospital was built on a hill and there was a high wall all the way round the building – a very high wall, but, because the hospital was built on a hill, you could stand in the grounds and look out to the countryside beyond. It gave an impression of not being closed in, but it must have been an unreal feeling for the patients, who could look out on the world but could not be part of it.

We went through later to where the women's quarters were, and where there was a unit where men and women worked together. It had just been set up and was being tried for the first time. The work was simple packing: outside firms sent in darts which they collected again when they had been packed. Initially there were some doubts about men and women working together, but it seemed to be working successfully. The men and women began to take a more personal interest in their appearance and their clothing.

There was a discothèque with a hi-fi in a brightly decorated room, and I heard that a well-known disc jockey used to go down regularly to officiate.

I was allowed to meet a girl who had once been in my care, and found her in the ladies' hairdressing salon, sitting under the drier and reading a book. At first she hid her face behind her book when she saw me, but then she talked for a while. I was quite surprised when she asked after one of the members of staff.

'You remember her?' I asked.

'Yes, I remember her well,' she said. 'She was all right.'

I asked after her parents, and one of the nurses showed me a large bouquet of flowers her parents had sent her. We talked for a minute or two, then I left. I was walking through a large sitting-room with my wife and one of the nurses, who was talking about the various activities they had at the weekend, when a young woman came up to me who looked to be in her thirties.

'You're Mr Hart,' she said.

'Yes, I am.'

'Don't you recognize me?'

I felt awful knowing I ought to have been able to say 'yes'. 'I'm sorry,' I said, 'I don't.'

'That's Mrs Hart, isn't it?'

'Yes. Do you know this lady?' I said to my wife.

'Yes. I know you, I think I know you.'

'I'm Ella,' she said smiling. 'I've dyed my hair, did it while I was on the run.'

'I'm sorry,' I said. 'Maybe that's it.'

'Do I look older?'

'Well, you do look older,' I said.

'But I'm not as old as I look.'

'How long have you been here?'

'Only a little while. You know why I came here, don't you?'

'No,' I said, 'I don't. I didn't know you were here, Ella.'

'Do you, Mrs Hart?' she asked.

My wife shook her head. 'No.'

'Come over here and sit down.' We went over to a settee and sat down with her and she talked about when she had been with us and all the places she had run away from. She was sedated, and at times was very quiet, giving the impression of having to concentrate very hard to be able to hold a conversation. We had to move on and, when she smiled, I caught a glimpse of the young woman of nineteen or twenty that she now was. When she stopped smiling it was as if another person stood there, someone ten years older. Her eyes were dull and her hair looked lank and uncared-for.

'Will you write to me?' she asked.

'Yes, if I'm allowed to.'

'Oh yes, you are allowed to.'

'You must drop me a line and let me know how you are, Ella.'

'Yes, I will.' She walked as far as the door of the sitting-room with us. 'It was so nice to see you.'

'It was nice to see you, Ella.'

'You look older,' she said to me, 'but *you* don't.' My wife laughed.

'Good-bye.' Ella came forward and kissed each of us on the cheek, then turned and walked back to the settee and sat down. She seemed tired and drained.

On the way home we didn't speak about Ella, but we both knew that we were thinking about her. Later that night my wife said, 'Ella . . .'

'Yes?'

'Do you know what she said to me before we left?'

'No.'

'She said, "They can't send me away from here, can they, Mrs Hart?" and I said, "No, they can't Ella," and she said, "And I can't run away from here like I did from the other places, can I?" and I said, "No." She said she never knew what she was running

144

from and she never thought she'd find her way there, but she was glad.'

'What did she mean by that?'

'She said she was glad there was nowhere else to run to.'

Some time later I heard that Ella had died. I remember the person phoning and telling me. 'It had to happen one day,' they said.

'I suppose so,' I said.

The verdict was suicide.

I could remember this still, quiet girl with the beautiful hair. I remembered the things she had said to me and I re-read the things she had written, particularly one piece of poetry.

> God's seesaw's a thousand miles long.
> I'll sit on one end
> Ride up and down
> High past the mountains
> Down through the town.
> God's foot's in the middle
> My hands will be free
> Happy and rejoicing
> Through eternity.
> Sitting on God's plank up in the sky
> Safe on the seesaw I'll be
> All the world
> Up there I shall see
> Safe on God's seesaw
> No longer lonely.

For so many children the seesaw of their lives has been one of unhappiness and fear. Perhaps everyone seeks a seesaw on which they can ride, feel the wind on their face and be able to look out over peaceful green fields with their hands free and without fear of falling. If Ella's seesaw is as long as she says, perhaps there will be room on it for all of us.

EPILOGUE

Each day in children's homes, in homes for the maladjusted and the subnormal and in community schools people meet to discuss children in their care. The majority of those caring for other people's children know that what they are doing is not enough, are aware of the deficiencies in the service and are equally aware of their own inability to meet the children's needs. They have to contend with staff shortages, low staffing ratios and the fact that people no longer want to do the job. Social workers in the field try to support families and prevent children coming into care, but often find the task almost impossible because of the pressures placed upon them by excessive case-loads – each morning when they enter their office they have to sort out three or four emergencies and give priority to the case that is most urgent.

Society seldom hears about the people who live and work in these homes. It has no knowledge of what they think or feel and seldom pays much attention to the social workers – the 'do-gooders' – who are caring for that section of society about whom the vast majority of the rest knows nothing: the deprived and displaced who wander from department to department within our social-service structure, seeking help, seeking comfort, seeking someone to talk to. But nobody listens, nobody really cares, or so it would seem to those of us who voluntarily take on the task of caring for other people's children. It is true that we don't have our arms twisted in order to do it, and there are those who say, 'Why bellyache when you take on a job only to find that it isn't what you thought it was going to be?'

A child was brought into a home in which I once worked, a child who had received a great deal of notoriety through the press. People living in the vicinity of the home got up petitions, wrote to the local M.P. and to the press demanding that she be removed. They did this because they were fearful about the welfare of their own children, and perhaps this was understandable. In their anxiety to have the child moved, all sorts of exaggerated statements were made with the intention of showing how unsuitable the home was to meet that child's needs and to protect their own children. 'Send her away, send her anywhere' . . . as long as she was cared for it was all right, but she must be cared for somewhere else.

Some time after the child had gone I was given a kitten which was not very bright intellectually. Having got itself up a tree fifty feet high, it discovered that there were no long branches for it to climb down. I approached the Fire Brigade, who informed me that they no longer had a service for rescuing pussies from high places, and then got in touch with the RSPCA who said that, 'What goes up must come down and when it is ready it will find its way down to earth.' Having sat under the tree making cat-like noises and holding up saucers of milk, all to no avail – I left it overnight. In the morning it was covered with frost and, feeling somewhat anxious, I again phoned the RSPCA, who told me not to worry about the frost, cats were given fur coats to keep out the cold. Two days and two nights he stayed up there, making quite piteous noises, and on the third day a reporter from the local press arrived. Someone had been complaining about our cruelty to a cat – the cruelty of leaving it up a tree. Our sense of values today seems to be as warped as that: get the child out, but let's not be cruel to the pussycat.

Homes and schools perhaps only become news when they are bad news, as hospitals for the subnormal are suddenly news when it is discovered that one of the patients has been ill-treated or has been left to sit around all day in only a pyjama jacket. The fact that two nurses may be caring for sixty adolescent, incontinent, mentally defective boys, changing their soiled sheets, washing their faeces-stained, urine-stained bodies – that is not news. People throw up their hands in horror about cruelty to such defenceless people, but how many of those who indignantly read the news in

148

the paper would want to go in and render assistance, let alone face up to the root causes of the problem?

When a child who is the responsibility of a local authority dies and an inquiry is held, the finger of blame is pointed at the social worker. Society's conscience is eased, for a scapegoat has been found . . . someone can be blamed, even though that social worker, overworked, deeply concerned and committed to her client, can only deal with one client at a time. She is expected to be clairvoyant, to be able to anticipate all that might happen to a disturbed human being in a disturbed household, and if she doesn't, society demands to know why. It is right to demand an answer, but there is little point in demanding answers if society itself is prepared to do nothing to ensure that the same thing cannot happen again – for happen again it will. The clients of social workers will die or be deprived of help – they will be deprived because there are simply not enough people to do the job.

So often the children I see, and the old people social workers tell me about, are not looking for experts – psychiatrists or experts in geriatrics – they are just looking for people . . . people who will devote their time, people who can convey, if only for a brief moment, their care and personal concern, who can help to deal with problems which often seem trivial to an outsider but which can be of overwhelming importance to a disturbed child or neglected old person.

The official staffing in children's homes is low, and staff shortages are acute throughout the country. This throws an extra burden on the men and women who care for these children. They, themselves, often begin to suffer from emotional and physical breakdown because of the pressures placed upon them. Social workers can often do no more than stagger from crisis to crisis when they should be able to deal systematically and compassionately with their caseload. Yet it is only when someone is damaged, hurt or dies because of our lack of insight, or when we have not actually gone out seeking trouble when so much trouble is already seeking us, that society takes notice. Then the social worker is no longer called a 'do-gooder', but a trained person who should have been able to do better. The same applies to a nurse, for nurses are not expected to ill-treat their patients any more than houseparents in children's homes are expected to indulge in acts of cruelty . . . but only when such things happen are these people noticed.

Then society, often through the popular or local press, condemns, points the finger, but still does not help.

Every citizen complacently believes that tragedies only happen to other people and that they themselves will never need the help of social workers or children's home staff or nurses in psychiatric hospitals or hospitals for the subnormal. But, sooner or later, it does happen to many more of us than we care to imagine: all those in difficulty today also once believed that it could never happen to *them*. There is no social or financial class that is immune.

The voices that cry out – those of social workers through their various organizations – try to draw attention to the needs of their clients, but often speak only to the converted; the vast majority does not hear them anyway. Those who work in children's homes and community schools, who see their children being failed by society and then punished by that society, know that so much more could be done if only there were enough people to do it. In the end, the quality of the care available is decided not by the social worker or the residential staff, but by society. Those in social service are the servants of society, their task to provide care for the sick and underprivileged section of that society. When they fail, it is society that fails, for they have been asked to do an almost impossible task while being denied the means with which to do the job.

We live in a ruthlessly competitive and acquisitive world. The wheels of commerce must be kept turning, people persuaded to aspire to and buy many things that they do not really need. The label 'success' can carry rich dividends, and the label 'failure' can be a suffocating handicap. Children sense all this from very early on in their lives. Meanwhile the traditional community support that existed in the original towns of the Industrial Revolution – as I glimpsed it in Oldham as a child – has been mostly dismantled with the old communities. This may have worked in a ramshackle, haphazard sort of way, but you'd need to be cynically complacent to claim we've yet replaced it with something very much better. Maybe that sort of support – from extended families and tight-knit neighbours – in fact solved very little, but it did give people something to live by at times when they had very little indeed.

The fact is, the 'failures' of the system are also the conscience of the system. A society such as ours owes a considerable debt to its casualties. But all too soon the 'failure' becomes the 'outcast', for that is how society seeks to keep itself free of guilt – and avoids paying the debt.

The people who seek out aid in the social services are not like the pussycat up the tree, perched on a branch, crying aloud and touching our hearts. They are hidden away – hidden away in institutions, or in the back room of some tenement, or lying on a park bench, or, as children, in a urine-stained bed with a depressed and suicidal mother unable to care – who has ceased to care anyway.

It is no use starting crying when society's servants fail their clients, when they fall short of the normally high standards they set themselves. It is easy enough then to ease the conscience and point the finger of blame. But it is not the social worker's social service, it is all of ours and it is as good as we are prepared to pay for. There is a deep need for a change of attitudes and priorities on the part of the public and its elected representatives, for it seems that only such a change will produce the means necessary to make the service adequate, if no more. Until society is prepared to think and feel and genuinely face the implications – and then give back some of what it has taken away in one form or another – there is little hope that the social services can become more than a desperately hard-pressed salvage operation, doomed to failure. We must ask ourselves *how we can afford that*.

Unless society cares enough by giving the social services the facilities to do their work adequately, the service will get worse – and it is getting worse. Fewer and fewer people are willing to work in homes for children, the aged or the mentally handicapped. The time of crisis is with us now. Even those who are there are leaving. And once they have gone, who will there be left to care?